NUTSHELLS

HUMAN RIGHTS LAW IN A NUTSHELL

AUSTRALIA
Law Book Co.
Sydney

CANADA and USA
Carswell
Toronto

NEW ZEALAND
Brookers
Wellington

SINGAPORE and MALAYSIA
Sweet & Maxwell Asia
Singapore and Kuala Lumpur

NUTSHELLS

HUMAN RIGHTS LAW
IN A NUTSHELL

SECOND EDITION

by

MAUREEN SPENCER,
Principal Lecturer in Law, Middlesex University

and

JOHN SPENCER,
Barrister

London • Sweet & Maxwell • 2004

Published in 2004 by
Sweet & Maxwell Limited of
100 Avenue Road, London, NW3 3PF
(http://www.sweetandmaxwell.co.uk)
Computerset by
Interactive Sciences Ltd, Gloucester
Printed in Wales by Creative Print & Design Group

No natural forests were destroyed to make
this product; only farmed timber
was used and replanted

A CIP Catalogue record for this book
is available from the British Library

ISBN 0–421–887400

©
Sweet & Maxwell
2004

CONTENTS

1. INTERNATIONAL HUMAN RIGHTS

THEORETICAL AND HISTORICAL DEVELOPMENT OF THE CONCEPT OF RIGHTS

Early development

"We hold these truths to be self-evident, that all men are created equal, that they are endowed by their creator with certain unalienable rights, that among these are life, liberty and the pursuit of happiness". Thus the American founding fathers set down in 1776 the essence of their conception of human rights. By today's standards the authors of the Declaration of Independence would be regarded as seriously deficient in their practice of human rights. Among them were wealthy slave-owners whose property included hundreds of other human beings, whose liberty and even life was at their mercy. This may suggest that the idea that people have rights by virtue of their humanity is historically conditioned and that human rights are a social construct whose content is not set in stone.

The content and extent of human rights are by their nature controversial. No-one has yet come up with an objective method of determining which asserted rights should be cherished and which should not. It is no longer fashionable to assume that the content of human rights can be derived from the essence of human nature as viewed by one or other of the world's religions. So human rights should not be regarded as forever fixed.

A living instrument

This is reflected in the way in which the European Convention on Human Rights and Fundamental Freedoms has been interpreted as a "living instrument" by the European Court of Human Rights in Strasbourg. Its Articles are not to be read so as to apply to them the intention of their original authors, but rather to give effect to their contemporary meaning. So social advances which improve the fundamental expectations of Europeans as to their basic rights will be incorporated into the Convention as they develop, though of course if public opinion becomes less liberal, the Convention might equally be interpreted more restrictively.

Teaching governments humanity

The history of the human rights concept is bound up with the revolutionary movements of the late eighteenth century, most notably the American and the French. Both revolutions sought their justification in the concept of natural rights. Against them stood the traditional view that the existing order had been divinely ordained and that people should only enjoy those rights which tradition or the benevolence of their rulers allowed. A crucial link between the American and French revolutions, Tom Paine, did a great deal to popularise the idea of human rights. His pamphlet "The Rights of Man" (1791) polemicised against monarchy and tyranny and demanded that governments be taught humanity.

The French Declaration of the Rights of Man (1793) contains the idea that because they are rights of the people, human rights stand higher than mere law. It stated: "Any law which violates the inalienable rights of man is essentially unjust and tyrannical; it is not a law at all. . . . Any institution which does not suppose the people good, and the magistrate corruptible, is evil".

Rise of the written constitution

With the rise of nationalism in the nineteenth century, written constitutions became the norm, and those of many countries, taking their example from the United States and France, incorporated references to basic or fundamental rights. England, by contrast, retained traditional forms of rule and adapted them to new times, without a written constitution, if we discount Magna Carta and the Bill of Rights 1688. Many streams of humanitarian endeavour have contributed to the development of a human rights culture internationally. One thinks particularly of the prolonged campaign for the abolition of slavery, the attempts to set down international rules for the conduct of war, and the movements for prison reform and the abolition of the death penalty.

Twentieth century developments

Another important strand is the de-colonisation of much of the world in the twentieth century. Most of the newly independent countries, for example in the British Commonwealth, adopted constitutions which detailed the human rights of their citizens. The success of some of these constitutions has helped to convince sceptical English lawyers and administrators of the virtue of legislating human rights, but perhaps the most important single impetus to the spread of human rights thinking was provided by World War II and its aftermath.

The Nuremburg trials

The Nuremburg trials, at which Nazi leaders were arraigned for crimes against humanity, set a key precedent. Despite its perhaps inevitable flaws, the process of bringing the fascist leaders to justice broke new ground. The leaders of what had been a sovereign government were being called to account for actions they had taken as a supposedly sovereign entity which were in breach of human rights.

United Nations Universal Declaration of Human Rights

In 1948 the United Nations adopted a Universal Declaration of Human Rights. Noting that:

> "disregard and contempt for human rights have resulted in barba-
> rous acts which have outraged the conscience of mankind, and the
> advent of a world in which human beings shall enjoy freedom of
> speech and belief and freedom from fear and want has been
> proclaimed as the highest aspiration of the common people",

the declaration set out a common standard of achievement for all peoples and all nations. Though it does not have the force of law it provides a yardstick by which the conduct of states and their governments can be judged.

The Universal Declaration was not adopted without conflict. Its form reflects the dominance of the western powers over the other states participating in the General Assembly discussion. The emphasis is on civil and political rights and it treats social and economic rights as of secondary importance. There is no mention, for example, of a right to self-determination, or the need of poorer countries for economic support. The final version of the Declaration dropped the right to petition which had featured in earlier drafts as an "essential human right". A right to resist oppression, which had been part of earlier drafts, also disappeared from the final version of the Declaration, on the somewhat tenuous ground that it could not be implemented by governments.

Other international human rights declarations

Regional declarations of human rights followed. The European Convention on Human Rights and Fundamental Freedoms was adopted by the Council of Europe in 1950. The convention was to be enforced by a European Court of Human Rights in Strasbourg, whose decisions would bind signatory governments. It is this document which has now been made part of English law by the Human Rights Act 1998. To give legal effect to rights and duties embodied in the Universal Declaration, the UN adopted an International Covenant on Civil and Political Rights, monitored by the UN human rights committee. It also adopted an International Covenant on Economic, Social and Cultural Rights (ICESCR), containing rights to work, social security, food, clothing and housing. The only absolute duty imposed on participating states, however, is to provide free primary education. States are supposed to work towards implementing the other rights recognised in the ICESCR to the maximum of available resources. Another important UN agency is the International Labour Organisation, originally formed in 1919 by the League of Nations, which has established minimum standards for conditions in the workplace, including rights to freedom of association and collective bargaining.

Other international human rights instruments include the Convention on the Status of Refugees (1951); the Convention on the Elimination of all forms of Racial Discrimination (1965); the Convention on the Elimination of all forms of Discrimination against Women (1979); the Convention against Torture and other Cruel, Inhuman or degrading Treatment or Punishment (1984) and the Convention on the Rights of the Child (1990). By adhering to these conventions, states commit themselves to safeguard the rights in question by their own laws and procedures. International supervision only becomes an issue when states fail to honour this obligation. In Europe, economic and social rights are protected by procedures established in the European Social Charter, adopted in 1961, which is intended to complement the European Convention on Human Rights. Like the ICESCR, it is drawn up in such a way as to make the realisation of social and economic rights an aspiration rather than a requirement and unlike the European Convention on Human Rights it has no enforcement mechanism.

British reluctance to incorporate the Convention

Most European states which have adopted the European Convention on Human Rights legislated to make its provisions part of their own law. Britain has been very late in doing so. This is in some ways rather surprising, because the Convention was actually drafted by a senior United Kingdom civil servant, and the UK was the first state to ratify the Convention. It was treated as a template for the constitutions of such former colonies as Nigeria, Bermuda, Cyprus and Malta.

There is a rich international experience of charters and bills of rights. Canada, Australia (and South Africa since the end of apartheid), countries where the common law prevails, have nonetheless embraced human rights legislation and built up case law on the basis of its application.

Categories of rights

The rights embodied in the European Convention on Human Rights fall into three broad categories. In the first are human rights, such as the right to life and the right not to be tortured or enslaved, which cannot be restricted under any circumstances. A second set of rights can be restricted only in time of war or public emergency threatening the life of the nation. Among these are the prohibition on forced labour, the right to liberty and security of the person and the right to a fair trial. The third category are rights such as the right to protection of private and family life, home and correspondence, freedom of expression, freedom of association and assembly, the right to marry and found a family, the right to property and the right to education. These rights are expressly subject to limitation, national governments being permitted to condition or restrict rights in this category in the interests of national security, territorial integrity, public safety or to prevent disorder and crime, or to protect health, morals or the rights of others. In each case the restriction must be both "prescribed by law" and "necessary in a democratic society".

Individual rights

Individual rights are strongly emphasised in the modern human rights movement. The right to life, the right not to be tortured or subjected to inhuman and degrading treatment, the prohibition on slavery, the right to a fair trial, not to be punished without law, to freedom of thought and freedom of expression, are quintessentially individual in their nature, and as rights they are founded on the humanity of the individual. They contrast with a second trend in rights thinking, which is concerned with the collective rights of peoples and social groups. International institutions such as the International Labour Organisation advance and enforce rights of employees and maintain internationally agreed legal standards in employment legislation.

The tension between individual and collective rights is substantial. Once-treasured arrangements, such as the trade union closed shop, seen as essential to maintain the rights of labour against powerful employers, have been undermined by their incompatibility with individual rights.

Collective rights

Collective rights are much less in evidence although the Convention does recognise rights to assembly and association. The archetypal human being envisaged by human rights law is the individual, in conflict with powerful institutions, chiefly the state itself and its emanations. In this model, the main danger of tyranny is seen to come from the state itself, whose power must be restricted as must that of any other institution which threatens to dominate at the expense of individual rights.

The first Protocol to the Convention in effect entrenches property rights. These cannot be infringed other than by the operation of law. This principle does not only operate to protect the rights and property of ordinary citizens. Recently the deposed former King of Greece won a ruling in the Strasbourg court entitling him to compensation for estates seized after he was forced into exile. The Convention is here acting as a brake on revolutionary expropriation and guaranteeing the property of magnates as well as small owners.

The movement to establish human rights has to be viewed as a global movement. Advances in human rights in one part of the world impact on other countries. Catastrophes like the collapse of former Yugoslavia and the genocide of Rwanda's Tutsi population generate a requirement for the application of universal standards of rights and justice, developing caselaw and materials which can be applied in the future. The scope and reach of human rights law has been advanced by the International

Tribunal dealing with crimes against humanity in former Yugoslavia, and by the tribunal which is dealing with the authors of the Rwandan genocide. There is now an International Criminal Court to deal with war crimes and crimes against humanity.

Civil liberties and human rights

The method of protection of rights and liberties in Britain has been different from most western democracies. In the first place there is no one constitutional document which provides the rules for the operation of the British constitution and the relationship between its various elements. As a corollary of this, before the Human Rights Act 1998, there was no equivalent to the United States Bill of Rights or the Canadian Charter of Rights. No document set out a range of rights which government, legislature and courts should enforce. Protection of civil liberties, such as freedom of speech, freedom of assembly and freedom from arbitrary arrest, was in the hands of Parliament and the courts through the common law. As a guardian of the people's interests, Parliament was expected to ensure that legislation did not unduly impinge on individual freedom. It was also expected that the courts, cherishing their independence from the executive, would interpret the law so as to allow the greatest freedom possible. Thus, to give one example, in *M v Home Office* (1993), the House of Lords confirmed that Ministers of the Crown are bound to obey court orders, in this instance not to deport an individual before his case could be heard.

There was however increasing unease that Parliament was gradually encroaching on liberties by a series of procedural pieces of legislation. These included, for example, the Prevention of Terrorism (Temporary Provisions) Act 1989, the Public Order Act 1986, limiting the freedom of assembly, and the Criminal Justice and Public Order Act 1994, which made inroads into the privilege against self-incrimination. It was not open to the courts to do other than apply the clear words of a statute even where this appeared to conflict with generally accepted civil libertarian principles. For example, in *Smith v Director of Serious Fraud Office* (1992) the House of Lords decided that important though the privilege against self-incrimination was, s.2 of the Criminal Justice Act 1987 had to be applied, even though its effect was to encroach on the privilege. Lord Mustill stated: "Neither history nor logic demands that any qualification of what parliament has so clearly enacted ought to be implied". General principles were secondary to the clear words of a statute. If there was no statutory intervention and the situation was governed by the common law there was less danger to civil liberties, particularly in relation to traditional liberal rights. In *Woolmington v Director of Public Prosecutions* (1935), the House of Lords determined that the burden of proof was always on the prosecution. A number of commentators including Keith Ewing and Conor Gearty in their book *The Struggle for Civil Liberties* (Oxford, 2000) have argued however, that the common law was less robust in protecting collective rights such as the right to assemble (see for example the Divisional Court decision in *Duncan v Jones* (1936), criticised by the Divisional Court in *Richmond-Bate v DPP* (1999)).

There are a number of statutes which enshrine positive rights in the UK, but these deal with specific practical areas of the law rather than posit general formulations. To cite one instance, the Police and Criminal Evidence Act 1984 sets out procedures for police investigations which are aimed at protecting the rights of those suspected or accused of crimes. For example, it specifies the right of access to legal advice in s.58. Such specific provisions exist alongside two jurisprudential approaches of the courts, namely drawing on international law as an aid to statutory construction in certain instances and deriving human rights principles from the common law.

The common law and human rights

The idea of human rights is foreign to the English common law. That is not to say that the common law does not share many of the values for which the human rights movement has campaigned, but the ruling principle of English law has for 300 years been the supremacy of Parliament, which naturally has been reluctant to cut down its own power. Parliament by enacting the Human Rights Act has ceded some of its power to the judges, who can at least in theory declare that Acts of Parliament violate human rights contrary to the Convention, although the Act in question remains operative. However, the judiciary in general have not been keen to wield their new powers in such a way as to place them at odds with the legislature. Anxious for an organic rather than a too rapid development of human rights law, judges have gone out of their way to discourage wide-ranging argument based on the Convention where the common law can provide an alternative route to the same end. Thus in *R. v North-West*

Lancashire Health Authority, Ex p. A (2000), heard on the eve of the coming into force of the Human Rights Act, the Court of Appeal criticised leading counsel for having tried to assert that where transsexuals were denied an operation to change their sex they were being subjected to cruel and unusual treatment, contrary to Art.3 of the Convention.

Lord Justice Buxton observed that Art.3 was concerned with positive conduct by public officials of a high degree of seriousness and opprobrium. To invoke it in the case before the court not only strained language and common sense, but seriously trivialised the Article in relation to the very important values it protected. The case was determined on classic public law principles, without reference to the Convention. And where possible in other cases judges have avoided using the Convention where an appropriate remedy is provided by the application of existing domestic law.

This is very characteristic of the English judiciary, which has frequently tended to treat extra powers as a burden rather than as a blessing. Something of a historical parallel is that when the Judicature Acts in the 1870s gave judges ostensibly unlimited powers to grant injunctions, the enabling Act was immediately interpreted so as to restrict the exercise of the injunctive power to cases where there was a pre-existing tort or breach of contract. On the other hand, where judges have seen a clear need to apply Convention standards to the administrative exercise of power, they have not hesitated to do so. A good example is *R. v Secretary of State for the Home Department, Ex p. Simms* (2000) in which a prisoner campaigning against his conviction complained that the authorities had refused to allow him to give press interviews. The House of Lords held that the limitations on the freedom of expression of prisoners had to be justified by pressing social need and as being the minimum interference necessary to achieve the objects of deprivation of liberty by a court and maintenance of order in prison. The prisoner had a legitimate interest in seeking to refer his case to the Court of Appeal and in enlisting the media to help him do that. There had been an unjustified curtailment of his human rights.

The individual and the state

Although making the Convention part of English law could thus be said to be an evolutionary rather than a revolutionary change, the Human Rights Act is having a profound impact on some areas of English law. In particular, it changes the relationship between the individual and the state, because it gives the victim of overweening state power an immediate domestic recourse to assert human rights. This in turn influences the way power is exercised right across the board. Courts and prisons have been the first to feel the effects, because here the imbalance of power between the subject and the state is at its sharpest. But like ripples across a pond, the effects are being felt throughout the system in time. However, students should realise that the Convention has been directly enforceable in the courts of most Council of Europe Member States for more than a quarter of a century. No doubt it has profoundly affected the legal systems of those countries, but, even now, none of the Member States is a human rights paradise with a flawless legal system.

2. THE EUROPEAN CONVENTION ON HUMAN RIGHTS

HISTORY

The European Convention on Human Rights is more than half a century old. It is a treaty of the Council of Europe, which was set up after World War II with the aim of re-establishing democratic government in Europe. At a meeting in the Hague in 1948 the Congress of Europe established the ten-member Council of Europe whose statute read: "Every member of the Council of Europe must accept the principles of the rule of law and the enjoyment by all persons within its jurisdiction of human rights and fundamental freedoms ... ". This founding statute was signed in May 1949. One of the main objectives of the newly-formed Council was to draft a human rights charter. The Convention for the Protection of Human Rights and Fundamental Freedoms was signed in November 1950 and entered into force on September 3, 1953. The treaty was largely drafted by UK lawyers, one of whom, Sir David Maxwell Fyfe, was subsequently a Conservative Lord Chancellor.

A minimum programme

Britain was one of the first members of the Council of Europe to sign up to the Convention and accept the jurisdiction of the Strasbourg-based European Court of Human Rights. But it was one of the last to incorporate the Convention into its domestic law.

Charters of rights usually have two characteristics. They represent a consensus among the drafters, so they are a minimum rather than a maximum programme, and they draw on a collective past experience, so they tend to aim at avoiding what has happened in the past rather than anticipating what may happen in the future. The European Convention is no exception. Sir Stephen Sedley has described it as essentially a nineteenth century set of rights. The Convention was intended as one of the instruments of post-war regeneration following the defeat of Hitler Germany. Fresh in the minds of the men who drew it up were the horrors of Nazi rule, the attempted extermination of the Jews, mass deportations, use of slave labour, police terror and state-sponsored political murder. Their main prescription to safeguard against any return to these terrible abuses was to entrench more strongly the liberal values such as rule of law and free speech which fascism (and communism in the USSR) had sought to overthrow.

In contrast to the vindictive Versailles treaty terms imposed on Germany and Austria by the victors of World War I, Europe after the Second World War was intended as a community of states committed to those values, and bound together by treaty to ensure that they were upheld. The chosen form was the Council of Europe, with an assembly and a committee of ministers, membership to be conditional on the acceptance of the rule of law and the enjoyment by all persons within the Member State's jurisdiction of human rights and fundamental freedoms. To codify those rights and freedoms the Member States drew on the recently adopted United Nations Universal Declaration of Human Rights, a rather vaguely-worded aspirational document, to put together a Western European declaration, intended to have legal force. The original thrust of the Convention was not to provide a forum for individual actions against government, but rather to provide a means by which states could keep one another up to the mark by mutually enforcing the domestic application of convention rights.

Political democracy and rights

The preamble to the Convention made it clear that an effective political democracy was equally as important as support for human rights in ensuring "justice and peace in the world". In addition the Member States had a collective responsibility for ensuring respect for the rights and freedoms in the Convention. This was realisable because the Council comprised "governments of European states which are like-minded and have a common heritage of political traditions, ideals, freedom and the rule of law". The set of rights embodied in the Convention has strong Cold War as well as post-war overtones. Individual rights are given much greater emphasis than what might be described as collective, economic, social and cultural rights. Social and economic rights are usually more controversial because they involve political choices about allocation of resources.

THE CONVENTION RIGHTS AND OBLIGATIONS: AN OVERVIEW

The Convention and positive obligations on states

Article 1

This requires that "the High Contracting Parties shall secure to everyone within their jurisdictions the rights and freedoms defined in Section 1 of this Convention". This may require positive steps by a government although the Court has recognised that "regard must be had to the fair balance that has to be struck between the competing interests of the individual and of the community as a whole". At the lowest level the requirement is to provide a legal framework to protect Convention rights effectively and at the highest to provide resources to individuals to prevent breaches. An example of the former is *Young, James and Webster v UK* (1980), where the court considered that Article 1 was violated in failing to protect the applicants from dismissal by British Rail because they were not in a union and the enterprise operated a "closed shop". The applicants thereby suffered a breach of their right to freedom of association under Art.11. It was not material that British Rail was a public body: "it was the domestic law in force at the relevant time that made lawful the treatment of which the applicants complained. The responsibility of the Respondent State for any resultant breach of the Convention is thus engaged ... ". In this case the court signalled that the state had responsibility for bringing in legislation which allowed a breach of Convention rights.

Cases where there has been a positive obligation to provide resources are rare. Article 6 may require the provision of free legal assistance and in *Airey v Ireland* (1979) this requirement was extended to the protection of rights under Art.8, namely family life. However, in *Burton v UK* (1996) the local authority had not violated Art.8 in failing to provide the applicant, who had cancer, with accommodation in a Romany gypsy encampment. The state has a more onerous duty to provide redress where fundamental rights are at stake, as in Arts 2 and 3.

Specific Convention rights

(a) Art.2. Right to life.
(b) Art.3. Right to be free from torture and from inhuman and degrading treatment.
(c) Art.4. Freedom from slavery and enforced labour.
(d) Art.5. Liberty of the person.
(e) Art.6. Right to a fair trial.
(f) Art.7. Freedom from retrospective punishment.
(g) Art.8. Right to respect for private and family life, home and correspondence.
(h) Art.9. Freedom of thought, conscience and religion.
(i) Art.10. Freedom to receive and impart ideas and information.
(j) Art.11. Freedom of association.
(k) Art.12. Right to marry and found a family.
(l) Art.13. Right to an effective remedy. (*N.B.*, not scheduled to Human Rights Act 1998)
(m) Art.14. Right to enjoy other Convention rights without discrimination.
(n) Protocol 1, Art.1. Right to peaceful enjoyment of possessions.
(o) Protocol 1, Art.2. Right to education.
(p) Protocol 1, Art.3. Right to free and fair elections.
(q) Protocol 4, Art.1. Prohibition of imprisonment for debt.
(r) Protocol 4, Art.2. Freedom of movement.
(s) Protocol 6, Art.1. Abolition of the death penalty.
(t) Protocol 6, Art.2. Death penalty in time of war.
(u) Protocol 7, Art.1. Procedural safeguards relating to expulsion of aliens.

    (v) Protocol 7, Art.2. Right to appeal conviction or sentence.

   (w) Protocol 7, Art.3. Right to compensation for victims of miscarriage of justice.

    (x) Protocol 7, Art.4. Right not to be tried twice for the same offence.

    (y) [Draft] Protocol 12. Right not to suffer discrimination. (Free-standing right not to be discriminated against, not yet in force.)

    (z) Protocol 13. Concerning the abolition of the death penalty in all circumstances.

ABSOLUTE, LIMITED AND QUALIFIED RIGHTS

	Articles	Protocols
Absolute rights	2, 3, 4, 13, 14	1(2)
Qualified rights	8–11	4(2)
Limited rights	5–7, 12	1(1), 7(2)

Some Articles establish unqualified rights and others contain a permitted list of exceptions. Article 18 states that the restrictions permitted under the Convention shall not be applied for any other purpose than those for which they have been prescribed.

Absolute rights

Articles 2, 3 and 4 are absolute—no exceptions are allowed. Articles 13 and 14 are without qualification. Protocol 1, Art.2, is absolute except that the state shall respect the right of parents to ensure such education and teaching is in conformity with their own religious and philosophical convictions.

Limited rights

Article 5 is limited. Everyone has the right to liberty and security of the person, save in six types of circumstances which are specifically listed. Article 6 is limited by implication. For example, some restrictions may be placed on access to the courts by prisoners (*Golder v UK* (1975)). However, restrictions must have a legitimate aim and be proportionate. Article 7 is limited in that it allows exceptions for crimes recognised under international law, primarily war-crimes. Article 12 is subject only to the require- ments that individuals seeking to marry are "of marriageable age" and they comply with marriage rules in domestic law. Protocol 1, Art.1, is only very narrowly limited. The right to peaceful enjoyment of possessions is conditional in that no-one may be deprived of his possessions except in the public interest and subject to the conditions provided for by law and by the general principles of international law. Protocol 7, Art.2, the right of appeal in criminal matters, may be subject to exceptions in regard to offences of a minor character, as prescribed by law or in cases where the person concerned was tried in the first instance by the highest tribunal or was convicted following an appeal against acquittal.

Qualified rights

Articles 8, 9, 10 and 11 are qualified rights in that they all allow limitations that are prescribed by law and are necessary in a democratic society. In addition each have a list of interests whose protection is compatible with the Convention. Protocol 4, Art.2, freedom of movement, contains a qualification along the lines of those in Art.8–11.

Article 8

The protected interests are:

    (a)   national security;
    (b)   public safety;
    (c)   the economic well-being of the country;
    (d)   the prevention of disorder or crime;
    (e)   health or morals; and
    (f)   the rights and freedoms of others.

Article 9

The protected interests are:

    (a)   public safety;
    (b)   public order;

(c) health or morals; and
(d) the rights and freedoms of others.

Article 10

The protected interests are:

(a) national security;
(b) territorial integrity;
(c) public safety;
(d) prevention of disorder or crime;
(e) health or morals;
(f) the rights of others;
(g) preventing the disclosure of information received in confidence; and
(h) maintaining the authority and impartiality of the judiciary.

Article 11

The protected interests are:

(a) national security;
(b) public safety;
(c) the prevention of disorder or crime;
(d) health or morals; and
(e) the rights of others.

PRINCIPLES APPLIED IN RESTRICTING CONVENTION RIGHTS

Two principles are common to all permitted restrictions. These are the principles of legality and proportionality.

Legality

This applies to the requirements of the phrases "in accordance with law" and "prescribed by law", as well as the word "lawful". The court will first assess whether there is a legal basis for the restriction. The court accepts that the exercise of discretion may be required but there must be sufficient indication of the circumstances in which the discretion will be exercised (*Silver v UK*

(1983)). Secondly, the rule restricting the Convention right must be accessible to the person or persons suffering the restriction. Thirdly, the restriction must be certain and reasonably foreseeable. However, as the Court put it in *Malone v UK* (1984): "The requirements of foreseeability cannot mean that an individual should be enabled to foresee when the authorities are likely to intercept his communications so that he can adapt his conduct accordingly". In *Hashman and Harrup v UK* (2000) the applicants, hunt saboteurs, had been bound over to be of good behaviour although their behaviour had not been found to be a breach of the peace. Their behaviour was *contra bonos mores*, behaviour seen as "wrong rather than right in the judgment of the majority of contemporary fellow citizens". The court did not accept that it must have been evident to the applicants what they were being ordered not to do for the period of the binding over. In view of the lack of precision the order was not "prescribed by law".

Proportionality

The test of proportionality relates to the application of the requirement for the restriction to be "necessary in a democratic society", implying the existence of a "pressing social need" (*Handyside v UK* (1976)). This concept is common in a number of jurisdictions. It means ascertaining whether a measure is necessary for the achievement of a legitimate aim and if so whether it fairly balances the rights of the individual and those of the whole community. The word itself does not appear in the text of the Convention. It is most often used in considering the restrictions of the rights under Art.8–11. The test is applied as follows:

- What is the "interest" which is relied upon? (These are listed in the Article).
- Does the interest correspond to a pressing social need?
- Is the interference proportionate to the interest?
- Are the reasons given by the authorities relevant and sufficient?

In other words it is for the authorities to convince the court that there is a pressing social need justifying the restriction and that the measures it has taken are proportionate to that need. There is a presumption that the restriction is not justified. (See also p.21).

Features of a "democratic society"

(a) The integrity of elections (*Bowman v UK* (1998) on election expenditure);
(b) "Pluralism, tolerance and broadmindedness" (*Handyside v UK* (1976)); and
(c) "Safeguarding democratic institutions" (*Klass v Germany* (1978) on secret surveillance).

However, it is important to realise that the court does not have a blueprint of a democratic society and will decide the issue on a case-by-case basis: "The court has to be satisfied that the interference was necessary having regard to the facts and circumstances prevailing in the specific case before it". (*Sunday Times v UK* (1979)).

Proportionality and other Articles

The test is also relevant to express restrictions under Arts 5, 12 and Art.1 of the First Protocol. In addition, it is applied in relation to implied restrictions which have been identified in Art.6. In *Ashingdane v UK* (1985) the court held that a limitation on the right of access to a court was not compatible with Art.6(1), if it does not pursue a legitimate aim and if there is not a reasonable relationship of proportionality between the means employed and the aim sought to be achieved.

DEROGATIONS

Under Art.15 a state may derogate from its obligations under the Convention "in time of war or other public emergency threatening the nation". This is only permitted "to the extent strictly required by the exigencies of the situation, provided that such measures are not inconsistent with its other obligations under international law". In other words, the Article is not to be invoked lightly. In *Lawless v Ireland* (1961) the applicant, a member of the Irish Republican Army, claimed that his detention was a violation of Art.5. The Irish government's specific measures of derogation were assessed by the court and it found that they could be characterised as measures strictly required by the "exigencies of the situation". The UK has registered derogations, mainly relating to Arts 5 and 6, both in relation to its colonies before independence and to Northern Ireland. It now has one derogation in place concerning pre-trial detention under the Prevention of Terrorism legislation (see *Brogan v UK* (1988)). In *Brannigan v UK* (1994) the applicant failed in a challenge to the UK's derogation from Art.5(3). The measures taken by the UK were proportionate (see also p.38). No derogations may be made from Art.2, except in respect of deaths resulting from lawful acts of war, or from Arts 3, 4 (para.1) and 7.

Death penalty

In July 2003 Protocol 13, ratified by the United Kingdom, came into force. This abolishes the death penalty in all circumstances, unlike Protocol 6 which allowed the death penalty in respect of acts committed in time of war or imminent threat of war. No derogations or reservations are allowed in respect of these Protocols.

RESERVATIONS

Article 64 of the Convention allows a state to enter a reservation when it ratifies an Article of the Convention if it considers that any law in force in that state is not in conformity with the Convention. The UK has entered a reservation with regard to Protocol 1, Art.2: the right to education. The court has held that a state may not make a reservation with regard to an Article of the Convention that does not deal directly with substantive rights and freedoms, but with procedure. In *Loizidou v Turkey* (1995) the court found that an attempt by the Turkish government to impose restrictions on the exercise of the right of individual petition and the jurisdiction of the court was impermissible.

JUDICIAL REASONING

The Convention rights are stated in general terms by contrast with the sort of detailed provisions which are to be found in much domestic legislation. Furthermore, the application of the Convention may require balancing a number of competing rights. For example, Art.8, the right to privacy, may conflict with Art.10, the right to freedom of expression. The method of interpretation adopted by the ECHR has involved the development of a number of analytical principles, which to some extent differ from the approach hitherto adopted by the English courts.

Textuality principle

The ECHR follows the provisions of Art.31(1) of the Vienna Convention on the Law of Treaties, which reads: "A treaty shall be interpreted in good faith in accordance with the ordinary meaning to be given to the terms of the treaty in their context and in the light of its object and purpose". The effect is that the court will look at the meaning of words within the textual and the social context of the Convention.

Teleological approach

The court adopts a teleological or purposive approach to inter-pretation, that is one that aims at realising its objects and purpose. An illustration of how the court manifests this approach is the case of *Golder v UK* (1979). The applicant, who was a prisoner, complained that he was not allowed to consult a solicitor on the possibility of bringing defamation proceedings against a prison officer who had accused him of being involved in a prison disturbance. After prison disciplinary hearings the prisoner was held not to have been involved. The court had to consider whether Art.6 included a right of access to the court and if so whether it had been violated in this case. The court considered that the "rule of law", which it was one of the purposes of the Convention to uphold, was inconceivable with-out the possibility of access to the courts. It commented:

> "This is not an extensive interpretation forcing new obligations of the Contracting States: It is based on the very terms of the first sentence of Article 6(1) read in its context and having regard to the object and purpose of the Convention, a lawmaking treaty and the general principles of law".

It is also part of the object of the Convention that its provision are interpreted in a way to make them effective. This was made clear in *Artico v Italy* (1981). There the court found a violation of the right to free legal assistance under Art.6(3)(c), where the government maintained that it was sufficient to appoint a lawyer to represent an applicant at his criminal trial and that it did not need to ensure that the lawyer attended the first day of the hearing. The court stated that "the Convention is intended to guarantee not rights that are theoretical or illusory but rights that are practical and effective".

Precedent

There is no doctrine of precedent under the Convention although the court will usually follow its previous decisions. On the contrary, the adoption of the principle of the Convention as a "living instrument" means that the Convention is to be interpreted in the light of changing conditions. This may mean that older decisions can be disregarded. For example, in a recent case involving the rights of transsexuals the court noted changing attitudes in this area (*Sheffield and Horsham v UK* (1999)) and compared it to the situation involving a previous case in *Cossey v UK* (1981):

> "Even if there have been no significant scientific developments since the date of the *Cossey* judgment which made it possible to reach a firm conclusion on the aetiology of transsexualism, it is nevertheless the case that there is an increased social acceptance of transsexualism and an increased recognition of the problems which post-operative transsexuals encounter. Even if it finds no breach of Article 8 in this case the Court reiterates that this area needs to be kept under review by the Contracting States".

Margin of appreciation

States are allowed some measure of freedom in applying the Convention. The doctrine of margin of appreciation is akin to that of "subsidiarity" in EU law, that is that the states' specific national traditions must be accommodated. The court addressed the issue in *Handyside v UK* (1976). A forfeiture order was obtained against *The Little Red Schoolbook* on the grounds that the publication of a book intended for children which included a section on sex contravened the Obscene Publications Acts 1959–1964. The applicant publisher argued that his rights under Art.10 were violated. The government claimed the restriction was necessary for the "protection of morals". The court took the view that the aim of the Obscene Publication Acts was legitimate, that is the protection of morals in a democratic society. The next issue was whether the restriction and penalties imposed were appropriate to the aim. Here the court had to decide how far it could go in interfering with the UK's margin of appreciation in this sphere. The book was legally available in Holland. The court pointed out that:

> " . . . the Convention leaves to each Contracting State, in the first place, the task of securing the rights and freedoms it enshrines . . .

These observations apply, notably to Article 10(2). In particular, it is not possible to find in the domestic law of the various contracting states a uniform European conception of morals. The view taken by their respective laws of the requirements of morals varies from time to time and from place to place, especially in our era which is characterised by a rapid and far-reaching evolution of opinions on the subject."

In the light of this the court did not consider there had been a breach of Art.10.

There is closeness between the concepts of proportionality and margin of appreciation. In *Gay News Ltd and Lemon v UK* (1982), the Commission considered the application of the law of blasphemous libel. It stated that: "It is in principle left to the legislation of the State concerned how it wishes to define the offence, provided that the principle of proportionality which is inherent in the exception clause of Art.10(2) is being respected". There was here no violation of the right to freedom of expression in a private prosecution against a publisher and editor for the vilifying of Christ in His life and crucifixion. The doctrine of margin of appreciation is particularly relevant to considerations of cases under Arts 6, 8 to 11 and Art.1, Protocol 1.

The Human Rights Act and the margin of appreciation

The doctrine is of course an international one and in principle should have no place in the consideration of the application of the Convention by national courts. Local courts are not required to declare local exceptionalism. In domestic law the doctrine of proportionality allows an assessment of the appropriateness of a policy decision by the executive (see p.17.)

INSTITUTIONS

The Commission on Human Rights

The original structure for the enforcement of the European Convention on Human Rights had a preliminary screening procedure, which was in the hands of a European Commission on Human Rights, based in Luxembourg. The Commission was empowered to receive from any state party to the convention any allegation of a breach of the convention by another state party. The Commission could also receive petitions from any person, group of individuals or non-governmental organisation claiming to be the victim of a violation of the Convention. In such cases, the Commission was charged to ascertain the facts and to place itself at the disposal of the parties to secure "a friendly settlement . . . on the basis of respect for human rights". Failing such a solution, the Commission was required to draw up a report, stating its opinion as to whether the facts disclosed a breach, and to recommend action to the Committee of Ministers, including referral of the case to the European Court of Human Rights. The Convention was amended by the contracting states with effect from November 1, 1998, so as to do away with the Commission and put all stages of the procedure for determining human rights applications in the hands of the Strasbourg court.

The Court of Human Rights

Article 20 of the Convention states that the number of judges of the European Court of Human Rights shall equal the number of states adhering to the Convention. The judges sit as individuals and not as national representatives, should be of high moral character and must "either possess the qualifications required for appointment to high judicial office or be jurisconsults of recognised competence". They are barred from undertaking any activity during their appointment which is incompatible with their independence, impartiality or the demands of full-time office. Appointment is by election by the Parliamentary Assembly of the Council of Europe, initially for six years, but may be renewed. The retirement age is 70. Judges can be dismissed by vote of two-thirds of their judicial colleagues if they cease to fulfil the conditions of office.

Structure

The court structure includes three different types of bodies, committees and chambers, and a Grand Chamber. The bulk of the court's work is carried out in chambers, each of seven judges. Committees, of three judges appointed from the chamber, have powers to strike out applications or declare them inadmissible. This preliminary sifting of applications was carried out by the Commission before 1998. Strike-out decisions taken by the committees are not appealable.

The chambers include as an *ex-officio* member the judge elected in respect of the state party whose conduct is being challenged, or a substitute nominated by that state. Should the case before it raise a serious question affecting the interpretation of the Convention, or be likely to result in a decision inconsistent with previous judgments of the court, the matter can, if none of the parties object, be referred to a Grand Chamber of 17 judges, which includes the President of the Court, his deputies and the Presidents of the Chambers. This court too must include an *ex-officio* member from the state whose conduct is impugned. A case can also be referred to the Grand Chamber after judgment at the request of one of the parties. Cases referred to the Grand Chamber under this provision are first sifted by a five-judge panel, whose decision to reject is not appealable. The Grand Chamber can also hear a request from the Committee of Ministers of the Council of Europe for an advisory opinion on "legal questions concerning the interpretation of the Convention and the protocols".

Legal regime

The legal regime of the Convention is based on the acceptance by the participating states of their obligation to secure human rights to all. States have the power to make certain reservations when they adhere to the Convention, or to derogate from some (though not all) of their obligations by lodging notice with the Council of Europe. All participating states are now obliged to recognise the right of individual petition to the court, though Turkey has attempted to limit its acceptance of the court's competence, stipulating that it was not prepared to allow petitions relating to the legal status of military personnel and military discipline and that the notion of a democratic society in Arts 8, 9 and 10 should be understood in accordance with the Turkish constitution. Not all the Member States have accepted these reservations. The Republic of Cyprus has also limited the commission's competence to review individual applications, so as to exclude those relating to the 1974 Turkish invasion and occupation.

Jurisdiction

The court has compulsory jurisdiction over all matters concerning the interpretation and application of the Convention which come to it by way of inter-state complaints, individual applications or on applications for a ruling on the interpretation of the convention. Applicants must have exhausted all domestic remedies and made their application within six months of the date those remedies were exhausted. Anonymous applications or applications concerning matters which have already been determined by the court or by some other international proceeding will not be entertained. Nor will the court consider applications incompatible with the Convention, or those that are manifestly ill-founded or an abuse of the right of application. Exhaustion of domestic remedies requires only that the applicant should have sought those domestic remedies available to him as of right, such as appeals to all available judicial bodies. It does not require that he seek a pardon. An applicant who is found not to have exhausted his domestic remedies may renew his application once he has done so.

Committee of Ministers and Secretary-General

The Committee of Ministers of the Council of Europe plays a part in the Convention procedure because of its power to request advisory opinions from the court and to supervise their execution. The members of the committee are the foreign ministers of all the states of the European Council, though the day-to-day work is usually done by their deputies, the ambassadors to the Council of Europe. Supervising the execution of court decisions includes ensuring that any awards made are paid, and ensuring that other actions required by the court are complied with, such as the passage or repeal of domestic legislation to conform with the Convention. The Secretary General of the Council of Europe is charged with keeping states informed of the names of ratifying or acceding states. If any state should denounce the European Convention on Human Rights in accordance with Art.58, it is the job of the Secretary-General to inform the other contracting parties.

Membership

Albania, Andorra, Armenia, Austria, Azerbaijan, Belgium, Bosnia and Herzegovina, Bulgaria, Croatia, Cyprus, Czech Republic, Denmark, Estonia, Finland, France, Georgia, Germany, Greece, Hungary, Iceland, Ireland, Italy, Latvia, Liechtenstein, Lithuania, Luxembourg, Malta, Moldova, Netherlands, Norway, Poland, Portugal, Romania, Russian Federation, San Marino, Serbia and Montenegro, Slovakia, Slovenia, Spain, Sweden, Switzerland, the former Yugoslav Republic of Macedonia, Turkey, Ukraine, United Kingdom.

ENFORCEMENT

The two distinctive features of the Convention were that its treaty provisions were legally binding on the High Contracting Parties and that it established a procedure for supervising the application of rights within each country.

Interstate petition

The original concept of the European Convention on Human Rights envisaged interstate petition as the main form by which actions would be brought before the Court. Article 33 of the Convention provides: "Any High Contracting Party may refer to the Court any alleged breach of the provisions of the Convention and the protocols thereto by another High Contracting Party". Examples of such actions include *Ireland v UK* (1978), concerning degrading treatment of prisoners in Northern Ireland; *Denmark v Greece* (1969), concerning torture under the colonels' dictatorship in Athens; and *Cyprus v Turkey* (1976), where the defendant state was found liable for rape of civilians by its soldiers. The number of such actions is small by comparison with the number of individual petitions to the court.

Individual petition

Article 34 (formerly Arts 25 and 46) provides that a High Contracting Party may accept the supervision of the Strasbourg court in cases where an individual, not a state, has taken a case. The Article allows the receipt of petitions from "any person, non-governmental organisation or group of individuals claiming to be the victim of a violation by one of the High Contracting Parties of the rights set forth in this Convention". Under Protocol 11, all states must accept the right of individual petition established under Art.34 and the compulsory jurisdiction of the court. This provision allowing individual petition of the court was not made compulsory until quite recently. Initially, the UK government refused to ratify the optional protocol. Other signatory governments, but not individuals, could bring actions against the UK under the Convention. The official explanation, given in 1958 by the then Foreign Secretary, Sir Reginald Ormsby-Gore, was that: "States are the proper subject of international law and if individuals are given rights under international treaties, effect should be given to those rights through the national law of the states concerned".

The compulsory jurisdiction of the court was unacceptable because it would mean British codes of common or statute law would be subject to review by an international court. However, that approach changed in 1966 when the government agreed that individual litigants could take their case to Strasbourg, if they were unable to establish through the domestic legal process the rights which the Convention gave them. If petitions were successful, the Human Rights Court could instruct the government to remedy the wrong they had suffered. But to exhaust their domestic remedies took a long time and to take a case on to the Human Rights Court cost on average £30,000. Only determined litigants could benefit.

Turkey is the only High Contracting Party to the European Convention to attempt to attach conditions to a declaration accepting the right of individual petition. This met with objections from a number of states and in *Loizidou v Turkey* (1995) the court held that it considered Turkey's acceptance of the right to individual petition to be unconditional.

Conditions of admissibility

Article 35 of the Convention requires that:

(1) the court may only deal with a matter after all domestic remedies have been exhausted, according to the generally recognised rules of international law and within a period of six months from the date on which the final decision was taken;

(2) the court shall not deal with any application submitted under Article 34 [Individual petition] that:
(a) is anonymous; or
(b) is substantially the same as a matter that has already been examined by the court or has already been submitted to another procedure of international investigation or settlement and contains no relevant new information;

(3) the court shall declare inadmissible any individual application submitted under Article 34 which it considers incompatible with the provisions of the Convention or the Protocols thereto, manifestly ill-founded or an abuse of the right of application; and

(4) the Court shall reject any application which it considers inadmissible under this Article. (According to Bailey,

Harris and Jones, *Civil Liberties, Cases and Materials* (1995), fewer than 10 per cent of applications are declared admissible).

THE CONVENTION AND UK LAW

The Convention and common law principles

British lawyers played an important part in the drafting of the text of the Convention and in doing so drew upon sources of English law including the writ of habeas corpus, the Magna Carta, the English Bill of Rights and the Act of Settlement. Although the British government long objected to incorporating the Convention, this was not because of its contents but because of the enforcement mechanism which would interfere with parliamentary sovereignty. It has been argued that the Convention is in essence a crystallisation of the common law and thus the common law itself provides adequate protection for human rights. On this argument the Convention simply enshrines tenets of classical civil liberties to be found in the history of English law. The courts have in the last three decades increasingly asserted that the Convention is declaratory of rights or principles which are to be found in the common law.

There are indeed a number of examples where the judges have shown themselves ready to articulate the law in terms of principles and of fundamental rights. In *Morris v Beardmore* (1981) for example, the House of Lords strictly construed a police constable's statutory power to require a person to submit to a breath test so as to render unlawful a request made by a constable who was at that time trespassing on that person's private property. Thus, the relevant power, contained in s.8(2) of the Road Traffic Act 1972, was interpreted so as to preserve the right to individual liberty along the lines of Art.5 of the Convention. An important series of cases on a prisoner's right of access to a court also illustrated this approach of the strict construction of wide discretionary powers (see *Raymond v Honey* (A.C. 1983); *R. v Secretary of State for the Home Department, Ex p. Anderson* (Q.B. 1984); *R. v Secretary of State for the Home Department, Ex p. Leech (No.2)* (Q.B. 1994)). In addition the courts have refined the standard of unreasonableness set out by the Court of Appeal in *Associated Provincial Picture Houses Ltd v Wednesbury Corporation* (1948). In *R. v Secretary of State for the Home Department, Ex p. Bugdaycay* (A.C. 1987), concerning an asylum application, Lord Templeman said that "where the result of a flawed decision may imperil life or liberty a special responsibility lies on the court in the examination of the decision making process". In *Derbyshire County Council v Times Newspapers* (A.C. 1993) the House of Lords held that a local authority did not have the right to sue for libel, reaching the decision "upon the common law of England without finding any need to rely upon the European Convention", *per* Lord Keith. The House considered that there was no difference between the common law of freedom of speech and Art.10. Interestingly, illustrating the increasing globalisation of judicial decision making, in that case the House drew in its reasoning on United States and South African authorities.

The Convention leads to changes in English law

Despite the limited access for UK litigants, the Convention had an impact on English law before the 1998 Act. Defeat in Strasbourg led to several pieces of legislation on such issues as the security services and telephone tapping. The UK assumed its treaty obligations to change the law so as to comply with rulings of the Court. For example, in *Sunday Times v UK* (1979) the court held that an injunction breached the paper's right of freedom of expression guaranteed by Art.10. As a result the UK amended its laws on contempt. More recently the decision in *Goodwin v UK* (2002) led to legislation to allow transsexual persons to marry in their acquired gender. (See p.95). Increasingly judges tried to harmonise decisions, particularly on judicial review, with the standards set by the Convention. Decisions of the Strasbourg court (in which judges from Britain participated alongside those of other European states) built up an influential body of human rights jurisprudence.

Judicial review

A powerful stimulus to the domestication of the Convention has been the growth of judicial review of administrative action in the domestic arena. This area of public law is very largely a post-war growth and its development has required extensive reform of the rules of court which in a previous period had served to keep the courts off ministerial backs. Though somewhat piecemeal, there is now a substantial experience of judicial scrutiny of government decisions, and the demarcation lines between the government and judicial spheres are much clearer. Judges have shown that they can act independently to apply concepts of fairness and justice to the process of administrative decision making, indirectly rebutting some of the objections of those who maintained they could not be trusted with people's rights.

International law

International law cannot override the clear words of a statute (see Ungoed Thomas J. in *Cheney v Conn* (H.C. 1968)). However it may be called as an aid to interpretation if a statute is ambiguous (see Lord Ackner in *R. v Secretary of State for Home Department, Ex p Brind* (HL 1991) and Lord Denning in *R. v Chief Immigration Officer, Ex p. Salamat Bibi* (CA 1976)). In addition the United Kingdom recognised the right of individual petition to the European Commission on Human Rights and the obligation to change the law so as to comply with human rights obligations under the European Convention on Human Rights. This was acknowledged by the Government in *Declarations Recognising the Competence of the European Commission of Human Rights to receive Individual Petition and Recognising as Compulsory the Jurisdiction of the European Court of Human Rights*, Cmnd. 2894. The Contempt of Court Act 1981 was passed as a result of the decision of the European Court of Human Rights that English law did not fulfil its obligations under Art.10 of the Convention on freedom of expression (see *Sunday Times v United Kingdom* (1974)). These obligations remain even after the implementation of the Human Rights Act. The status of the European Convention on Human Rights in English law was changed as a result of the Human Rights Act but the status of other Treaty Conventions remains the same. In practice however, they are far less often at issue.

3. THE HUMAN RIGHTS ACT 1998

The Act received the Royal assent on September 9, 1998. The purpose of the Act is to give further effect to the rights and freedoms guaranteed under the European Convention on Human Rights. However, it is important to underline that the Act does not incorporate the Convention into domestic law in the way that the European Communities Act 1972 incorporates the

Treaty of Rome. What the Human Rights Act does is to give certain provisions of the Convention and its Protocols a defined status in English law. In effect it creates a new constitutional statutory tort only applicable to public authorities when they breach rights enshrined in certain provisions of the European Convention on Human Rights. It also requires that existing rights and obligations, including those under statute, should be interpreted in a way which is consistent with the Convention. It is a matter of lively ongoing debate however, whether the Act allows the Convention rights to create new private law causes of action under English law. The Act specifically acknowledges the principle of parliamentary sovereignty by providing that, where a court decides that a legislative provision in incompatible with the Convention, "a declaration of incompatibility" may be made but it is then for Parliament to decide whether the provision should be changed.

THE DEBATE ON THE HUMAN RIGHTS ACT

The pressure for incorporation

Partly because it delayed incorporation longer than most other European states, the UK lost more cases in Strasbourg than any other country except Italy. The Blair government thought this was a powerful argument for incorporation, but the high figure was not surprising given that only Strasbourg could resolve disputes between English law and the Convention. Such disputes were inevitable given the spread of government functions and its intrusion into more and more spheres of life.

Governments of both persuasions were in practice reluctant to take the radical step of incorporation. Labour's Green Paper on the subject in 1976 came to nothing. Prime Minister Thatcher took the view that one Bill of Rights, the one dated 1688, was enough, though a Conservative backbencher, Sir Edward Gardner Q.C., brought in a private member's bill for incorporation. Lord Lester Q.C., a Liberal Democrat peer, waged a long campaign in the House of Lords in favour of bringing the Convention into domestic law. When John Smith became leader of the Labour Party he pledged that a future Labour government would do so. Outside parliament, the proposal was gathering support within the legal profession and the judiciary and from organisations such as Charter 88, set up to highlight what were perceived as the UK's constitutional deficiencies, and Liberty, the re-launched former National Council for Civil Liberties, once closely associated with the Communist Party but committed in the 1990s to advocacy of liberal values. The vogue for human rights can be seen as a move away from the search for radical or revolutionary political solutions in favour of clipping the claws of the modern state without disturbing the existing social and property relations.

The success of the Convention

Perhaps the most persuasive argument for incorporation was the long-term success of the European Convention itself. Until the 1970s the convention remained "a sleeping beauty", in the words of a former Vice-President of the European Human Rights Commission. The floodgates began to open with the spread of the right of individual petition. By 1997 the Commission had dealt with almost 40,000 individual petitions, and the court was working flat out to deal with a growing backlog of individual cases. The arguments which raged for and against the introduction of the Human Rights Act are set out below since they provide a framework with which to assess the impact of the legislation. (See also pp.151–155).

Counter-arguments

Among the arguments deployed against domesticating convention rights was that human rights were adequately protected by the common law (see for example the House of Lords decision in *Derbyshire County Council v Times Newspapers Ltd* (1993)). This view was repeatedly contested by, among others, the United Nations Human Rights Committee. Its 1995 report, for example, stated flatly that the UK system "does not ensure fully that an effective remedy is provided for all violations" of rights under the UN human rights covenant. While some opponents of incorporation argued that judges were quite capable of protecting rights through the common law, others, led by Professor John Griffith, argued that to place the power to enforce convention rights in the hands of unelected judges would undermine democratic participation and detract from accountability.

To a large extent the debate on incorporation of the Convention, in the last decade of the twentieth century, amounted to a critique of the constitution as a whole. Not all the protagonists on each side agreed with each point but the principal arguments which were then put were:

In favour of incorporation

(a) existing common law safeguards had failed;

(b) the discussion on implementation would have the beneficial effect of raising public awareness of the issues;

(c) judges would be constrained to follow principles which were generally agreed; many issues which are of general human concern would be removed from constant change precipitated by party politics;

(d) The United Kingdom would be following the example of many other countries that have found it valuable to implement a bill of rights;

(e) strict party discipline means that parliament does not act independently to check the executive, so a Bill of Rights was needed to deal with what Lord Hailsham called an "elective dictatorship";

(f) recourse was already available to Strasbourg, and it would simplify matters for litigants if there was a national court capable of dealing with these issues.

Against incorporation

(a) its content would be too general and vague, and there would be a constant battle over what should be included, for example, controversial matters such as the right to picket;

(b) the judges would interpret the legislation too narrowly and would have increased power to impose their class-based view of rights;

(c) society is based on a conflict of interests and, on the whole, it would be impossible to satisfy these impartially: it is better that they be debated politically rather than legally;

(d) the record of the Strasbourg court on certain matters —trade union rights at Government Communication Headquarters, for example—is a cause for concern; collective as opposed to individual rights are badly protected;

(e) it would encourage too much litigation;

(f) legislative change would be continually delayed by constitutional conflict, as has happened in Canada, for example;

(g) human rights were already well protected in the UK: contrast this with other countries, such as the former USSR, where a Bill of Rights or its equivalent did not prevent gross abuse;

(h) incorporation would be against the pragmatic British approach to problems;

(i) a Bill of Rights would not be compatible with the doctrine of parliamentary sovereignty and entrenchment would be impossible; without entrenchment the Bill would have only moral force;

(j) the common law adequately protected human rights and accepted the principles enshrined in the European Convention.

THE HUMAN RIGHTS BILL

The constitutional implications were summarised by the Lord Chancellor, Lord Irvine, in introducing the Human Rights Bill in the Lords in 1997:

> "The traditional freedom of the individual under an unwritten constitution to do himself that which is not prohibited by law gives no protection from misuse of power by the state, nor any protection from acts or omissions of public bodies which harm individuals in a way that is incompatible with their human rights under the convention".

The Bill was a compromise between a number of different standpoints. Some unsuccessfully argued for an Act which would be constitutionally entrenched, like the first ten amendments to the Constitution of the United States. Another rejected model was that of the Canadian Charter, which prevails over inconsistent primary legislation unless it employs a "notwithstanding" clause making it clear that the intention was to legislate inconsistently with the right in question and in such a case the inconsistent legislation survives. However, it was considered that entrenchment and judicial review of primary legislation were less desirable than the retention of parliamentary sovereignty and the separation of powers between parliament and the judiciary. The Labour Party in opposition produced a consultation document, *'Bringing rights home'*, and included a commitment to incorporate the Convention in their manifesto. After the May 1997 election the Labour government published a White Paper: *Rights Brought Home, the Human Rights Bill*. The Bill was introduced in the House of Lords on October 23, 1997. Some remained sceptical. Lord McLuskey in the debate in the House of Lords anticipated that the Act would provide "a field day for crackpots, a pain in the neck for judges and legislators and a goldmine for lawyers". In the Lords it met opposition from the Church of England and the press, worried about the effect of the Bill on their autonomy. Amendments were introduced which went some way to satisfy their concerns.

The press

Section 12 of the Human Rights Act provided that courts or tribunals considering whether to grant relief which might affect the exercise of the right to freedom of expression must have particular regard to the importance of that right. In relation to journalistic and literary or artistic material or conduct, the court or tribunal must take account of the extent to which the material is or is about to be available to the public and the public interest in publication, together with the terms of any relevant privacy code such as that set out by the Press Complaints Commission. In provisions which change the procedure in which courts approach applications for interim relief, such as that in *Spycatcher*, and for orders restraining reports of legal proceedings, the Act specifies that relief may not be given against a person who is neither present nor represented in court, unless the court is satisfied that the applicant has taken all reasonable steps to notify the person or that there are compelling reasons for not notifying them. No interim order restraining publication can be granted unless the court is satisfied that the applicant is likely to establish at trial that publication should not be allowed.

The Church

One of the fears of the Church was that the Act might undermine their refusal to marry gay couples or dismiss teachers who had abandoned Christianity. Section 13 of the Act provides that if the court's determination of any question under the Act might affect the exercise by a religious organisation or by its members collectively of the Convention's right to freedom of thought, conscience and religion, special regard must be had to the importance of that right.

Capital punishment

In the House of Commons there was added to the list of Convention rights, on a free vote, the right to be free from capital punishment in peacetime (this prompted the UK government to ratify the Sixth Protocol in January 1999).

Royal Assent

The completed Bill received the Royal Assent on November 9, 1998. It came into force on October 1, 2000 after a legal training programme for judges and tribunal members costing more than £4,500,000.

The main provisions of the Human Rights Act

The Convention rights

The Act nowhere states that the Convention rights are incorporated or that all UK citizens now have the rights set out in the Convention or even that its purpose is to achieve these two objectives. Section 1 and Sch.1 of the Act list the Convention rights which are included in the Act. The rights which are to have effect under the Act are those contained in:

(a) Arts 2 to 12 and 14 of the Convention;
(b) Arts 1 to 3 of Protocol 1;
(c) Art.1 and 2 of Protocol 6.

Excluded Articles

Significantly, Art.1 is not incorporated. This Article imposes a duty on the states that have ratified the Convention, to "secure to everyone within their jurisdiction the rights and freedoms" protected by the Convention. It is on one level understandable that it was not included, since it simply reiterates the responsibility which the government has assumed in passing the Act. However there is no section placing a positive duty on the state to ensure that domestic law is compatible with Convention rights. This has important implications for the obligation to uphold Convention rights in the private law sphere. The European Court of Human Rights has in a number of cases imposed a responsibility on states for violations by private bodies by citing Art.1. Thus in *Young, James and Webster,* the law governing the relationship between private parties (in relation to the closed shop) was in breach of Art.11 (freedom of association) and in addition the state had a responsibility via Art.1 to regulate this law. The possibility of a claim for a remedy against the state being made is ruled out by the omission of another key Article, Art.13. The Home Secretary explained in Committee:

> "We took the view that the best way of applying Article 13 in the context of incorporating the Convention was to spell out in specific clauses how those remedies should be made available. Therefore we take from Article 13 that 'Everyone whose rights and freedoms . . . are violated shall have an effective remedy' and then set out in the Bill what whose effective remedies should be and how they can be accessed".

The main difference between the provisions, however, is that Art.13 gives a right to a remedy in unlimited terms, whereas s.8 of the Human Rights Act limits remedies to cases involving "act[s] (or proposed act[s]) of a public authority". Thus remedies are not available because of actions or omissions by the state itself or by private bodies (see Ch.9).

Excluded Protocols

Protocol 4 has not been ratified by the UK. The reason is a conflict between the British Nationality Act 1981, which denies entry to some UK nationals, and Art.3 which covers rights of entry of nationals. Protocol 7 is also not included.

Derogations, National Security and Terrorism

Section 1(2) of the Act provides that the Articles which are covered by the Act are subject to any "derogations" under Art.15. This states that:

> "In time of war or other public emergency threatening the life of the nation any of the High Contracting Parties may take measures derogating from its obligations under this Convention to the extent strictly required by the exigencies of the situation".

The UK Government has used this Article to avoid its responsibilities in relation to Northern Ireland (see *Brogan v UK* (1988) and

Brannigan v UK (1993)). Section 14 of the Act lists "designated derogations" which can be continued for up to five years. Under s.14(5) the Secretary of State may amend s.3 of the Act to extend existing derogations and add any new one. In fact, the Terrorism Act 2000 creates a new procedure for detaining and questioning terrorist suspects and the derogations may no longer be needed.

Under s.14(5), the Secretary of State may amend s.3 of the Act to extend existing derogations and add any new ones. The introduction of judicial authorisation for extended detentions in the Terrorism Act 2000 allowed the existing derogation to be withdrawn in February 2001. The interaction between human rights and terrorism has become an important legal question. Recent legislation including the Terrorism Act 2000 and the Anti-Terrorism Crime and Security Act 2001 has significantly widened the legal definition of terrorism and expanded the powers of the government, police and security services. The 2000 Act defines terrorism in broad terms as the use or threat of action anywhere in the world involving serious personal violence, serious damage to property, endangering of life or creating serious risk to health and safety or designed seriously to interfere with or seriously to disrupt an electronic system. The act must be designed to influence a government or to intimidate the public or a section of the public anywhere, and its use or threat must be made for the purpose of advancing a political, religious or ideological cause. A number of groups considered to come within this definition are specifically proscribed by the Act. It gives police enhanced powers to investigate terrorism, including wider stop and search powers, and the power to detain suspects after arrest for up to seven days (though any period longer than two days must be approved by a magistrate). Three of the original proscribed organisations sought judicial review of their proscription *in R. (on the application of the Kurdistan Workers Party) v Secretary of State for the Home Department* (2002) Judicial review was not the appropriate route, the Divisional Court decided. The proper route was an application to the Home Secretary to deproscribe, followed if necessary by an appeal to the Proscribed Organisations Appeal Commission. *Re Attorney General's Reference (No.4 of 2002)* (2003) concerned the burden of proof of membership of a proscribed organisation. In effect s.11 of the 2000 Act requires a suspect to prove either that the organisation was not proscribed or that he has not participated in its activities while it was proscribed. The court held that this placed a legal, not an evidential burden on the defendant which might be contrary to the presumption of innocence under Art.6(2) of the Convention, but was in any event justified and proportionate. The 2000 Act creates new criminal offences of inciting terrorist acts, seeking or providing training for terrorist purposes at home or overseas, and overseas, and providing instruction or training in the use of firearms, explosives or chemical, biological or nuclear weapons. The Anti-Terrorism Crime and Security Act 2001 passed through parliament in the aftermath of the September 11 atrocities in the United States. It widens still further the powers of the authorities to act against terrorism and introduces internment for foreign nationals suspected of terrorist involvement, where human rights considerations do not permit their deportation. This provision involves an explicit derogation from Art.5 of the European Human Rights Convention, which would otherwise have the effect of limiting the time under which a person facing deportation could be held and would not allow further detention without charge or trial where a deportation was no longer being pursued. The provisions may eventually be challenged in Strasbourg where the issue is likely to centre on whether the circumstances under which the legislation was introduced were a "war or other public emergency" under Art.15. The English courts have already decided this issue in the government's favour: see *A v Secretary of State for the Home Department* (2002). The Special Immigration Appeal Tribunal set up by statute with jurisdiction over all immigration and asylum cases concerning national security issues considered the detention of 11 suspects under the ATCSA in July 2002. They challenged the detention claiming the derogations was unlawful and did not meet the requirements of Art.15(1). They claimed that the government had not established "a public emergency threatening the life of the nation"; secondly that even if there was such an emergency the detention was a disproportionate response and thirdly that the detention was inconsistent with Art.14 in that it was discriminatory on grounds of nationality. SIAC held in favour of the third but not the first two grounds. They indicated that there were potential grounds for a derogation but it should be extended to all suspected international terrorists. The Home Secretary's appeal was upheld by the Court of Appeal. In 1999, SIAC had upheld the appeal of a Pakistani national refused indefinite leave to remain in the UK because he was believed to be a danger to national security. It considered the expression "national security" had been drawn too widely. The Court of Appeal and the House of Lords upheld the Home Secretary's appeal. Lord Slynn of Hadley stated that the Home Secretary was "undoubtedly in the best position to judge what national security requires". However, in a later case the Court of Appeal supported SIAC's decision. In *Secretary of State for the Home Department v M* (2004), the Court of Appeal upheld a Tribunal decision quashing the detention of a Libyan national under the Home Secretary's new powers. The Home Secretary was refused permission to appeal. The 2001 Act also gives the police powers to freeze terrorist assets on suspicion. Both Acts are subject to special review procedures. The workings of the 2000 Act are reviewed annually by an independent reviewer, Lord Carlile of Berriew Q.C., who also reviews the internment provisions of the 2001 Act. A committee of Privy Councillors, headed by Lord Newton of Braintree, reviewed the whole of the Anti-Terrorism Crime and Security Act 2001 and its report criticised many of the provisions of the Act. It strongly recommended that the powers which allowed foreign nationals to be detailed indefinitely should be replaced as a matter of urgency. It said new legislation should deal with all terrorism, whatever the origin of nationality of its suspected perpetrators, and should not require a derogation from the European Convention on Human Rights. The Home Secretary undertook to consider carefully the report's recommendations. Reported in December 2003.

Section 15 of the Human Rights Act contains the concept of "designated reservations". A reservation is a concept in international law which allows a state which is signatory to a treaty to reserve particular laws or policies in order to exempt them from any challenge. Reservations are made at the time of ratification but amendment to the Convention by a new Protocol allows new reservations. The UK has reserved the second sentence of Art.1 of Protocol 1, which requires education to be provided in conformity with parents' religious and philosophical convictions. It is accepted only so far as it is compatible with the provision of efficient instruction and training and the avoidance of unreasonable public expenditure.

Interpretative provisions

The first way by which the Convention impacts upon domestic law is through the obligations in respect of statutory interpretation in s.3. This requires that "so far as is possible to do so", both primary legislation and delegated legislation are to be read and given effect to in a way which is compatible with Convention rights. This appears to amend the position set out by the House of Lords in *R. v Brown* (1994) which limited the use of the Convention as an aid to interpretation to statutes which were "post Convention and ambiguous". In that case the courts were not required to interpret the Offences Against the Person Act 1861 in a manner consistent with Convention rights in the prosecution of a number of men who had been willing participants in sado-masochistic activities. Section 3 states that the obligation applies to "primary legislation and subordinate legislation whenever enacted". However, the section stresses that if primary or sub-ordinate legislation is incompatible with a Convention right and it is not possible to construe the former to meet the demand of the latter, the legislation prevails.

Included within the definition of primary legislation are pre-rogative orders. This has the effect of narrowing the scope of the application of the decision of the House of Lords in *R. v Minister for the Civil Service, Ex p. Council of Civil Service Unions* (1986), that certain acts of the prerogative were judicially reviewable. Prerog-ative orders prevail if in conflict with Convention rights. The House of Lords ruling would still apply to other litigation such as judicial review and challenges in the criminal courts where the ground of complaint is not incompatibility with a Conven-tion right. The Act specifically preserves the validity of all legislation that is inconsistent with Convention rights. Geoffrey Marshall has argued (*The Times*, January 27, 1998) that this latter provision gives the "United Kingdom a defective measure that will put it at the bottom of any international Bill of Rights league table".

Section 2 requires that a court or tribunal determining question which arises in connection with a Convention right must take into account the judgments, decisions, declarations or opinion of the European Court of Human Rights and the Commission. This means that the Strasbourg case law has a more influential status but is still not binding. An example of the effect this may have is provided by the contrasting decisions of the "gays in the mili-tary" case, *R. v Ministry of Defence, Ex p. Smith* (1996): the Divisional Court and the Court of Appeal considered the Stras-bourg jurisprudence but failed to follow it because it was not part of domestic law. However, in *Smith and Grady v UK* (2000) the European Court of Human Rights found that the exclusion of homosexual service personnel contravened Art.8 of the European Convention.

One effect of ss.2 and 3 is that the Strasbourg method of judicial reasoning has increasing effect in English courts. The approach of the English courts to precedents will be affected. It is often stressed that the Convention "is a living instrument which . . . must be interpreted in the light of present day conditions" (see *Tyrer v UK* (1978)). The duty is thus to take account of the Strasbourg case law, not necessarily to follow it. On occasions it may be possible indeed that the English courts will actually surpass the Strasbourg jurisprudence in developing concepts of rights. An indication of this possibility is to be found, for example, in *Fitzpatrick v Sterling Housing Association* (1999), where the House of Lords found that as a matter of English law a stable gay relationship was a family, thus enabling the surviving partner of a homosexual to retain a lease on a council flat. This was despite the fact that Strasbourg had not to date accepted that gay relationships were the basis of a family.

Proportionality

Proportionality can now constitute a ground of judicial review, at least in cases brought since the Human Rights Act 1998 came into effect. *R. (Daly) v Secretary of State for the Home Department* [2001] arose from a complaint by a serving prisoner against a search of his cell in his absence which involved the prison authorities reading legally privileged correspondence. The House of Lords held that the prisoner retained the right to communicate confidentially with his legal advisers. The practice complained of was not necessary for the prevention of disorder or crime and was accordingly disproportionate. Proportionality is also a principle of European Community law which binds the English courts. In *R. v Secretary of State for the Environment, Transport and the Regions, Ex p. Holding and Barnes (Alconbury)* (2001), Lord Slynn said: "I consider that even without reference to the Human Rights Act the time has come to recognize that this principle [proportionality] is part of English administrative laws, not only when judges are dealing with Community Acts but also when they are dealing with acts subject to domestic law." The limits of the application of this principle were shown in *R. (Association of British Civilian Internees: Far East Region) v Secretary of State for Defence* (2003). The Court of Appeal dismissed an appeal by an association representing civilian detainees interned during World War II by the Japanese. In 2000 the government had announced that £10,000 would be paid to British civilian victims of Japanese internment. But in July 2001 it was announced that compensation would only be paid to internees who had been born in the UK or who had a parent or grandparent born in the UK. The association sought judicial review of the restriction on the grounds that it was disproportionate or irrational and defeated legitimate expectations aroused by the original announcement. The question arose whether proportionality was the appropriate test where the claim for judicial review raised no human rights issues. The Appeal Court held that in such cases proportionality had not replaced the traditional test of reasonableness. Though the original announcement had lacked clarity it did not constitute a clear and unequivocal representation that all interned British subjects would qualify so the government had not violated a legitimate expectation.

Statements of compatibility

Section 19 provides a presumption that future legislation should read to be compatible with the Convention. It provides that when legislation is introduced in parliament for a second reading, the minister introducing the Bill must either make a statement to the effect that in his or her view the legislation is compatible with the Convention or make a statement to the effect that although the legislation is not compatible with the Convention the government still wishes to introduce it. The Human Rights Act is thus like the Interpretation Act 1978 in that it set out a framework which shapes the interpretation and implementation of other legislation, both before and after the passing of the Act. It is of course more than an interpretative Act in that it also sets out a set of principles which are given important but not overriding status.

Declarations of incompatibility

Under s.4 a court which is satisfied that a provision is incompatible with Convention rights has to make a declaration of incompatibility. This is only possible in the higher courts, namely the House of Lords, the Privy Council, the Court of Appeal and the High Court. A declaration does not affect the continuing validity of the provision in question. If the matter of a declaration of incompatibility is raised in proceedings to which the Crown is not party, the Crown is entitled to notice of such a declaration and may be joined as a party to the proceedings (s.5). It will not be possible for an individual to take a suit against the executive for failing to introduce a piece of legislation as s.6(6) specifically provides that a failure to introduce legislation or a remedial order is not included.

Judicial deference

Some commentators have bemoaned what they claim is a reluctance of the judiciary to employ the Human Rights Act effectively to challenge the power of the executive and the legislature. Declarations of incompatibility have been rare, the courts seemingly reluctant to be seen to suggest that parliament should change the law. On occasion the courts have taken a creative approach to legislation, for example, interpreting the rape shield provisions of s.41 of the Youth Justice and Criminal Evidence Act in _R. v A_ (2001). The House of Lords, in a majority decision, avoided making a declaration of incompatibility taking the view, advocated by Lord Steyn, that unless "a clear limitation on Convention rights is stated in terms" the court could interpret an Act compatibly with the Convention. The view of the minority was that this turned the will of parliament on its head. Significantly, the right at stake here was the right to a fair trial, Art.6, where the judges have generally taken a more activist stance. By contrast in _Brown v Stott_ (2001), the Privy Council adopted a more cautious approach considering that the public interest in enforcing drink-driving legislation had to be balanced against the right enshrined in Art.6. In _Bellinger v Bellinger_ (2001) the House of Lords, declined to stretch the interpretation of the statute, held that the recognition of gender reassignment for the purposes of marriage was for legislation not the judiciary. It granted a declaration of incompatibility. In _Wilson v First County Trust Ltd (No.2)_ (2001) the House of Lords took the view both that it had no jurisdiction to make a declaration of incompatibility concerning events that predated the enforcement of the Human Rights Act and also that the concept of proportionality should be restrictively applied. Lord Nicholls stressed that the courts had a "reviewing role". He continued, "Parliament is charged with the primary responsibility for deciding whether the means chosen to deal with a social problem are both necessary and appropriate. Assessment of the advantages and disadvantages of the various legislative alternatives is primarily a matter for Parliament." Again in _Re W & B (Children: Care Plan)_ (2001) the House held that the Court of Appeal had exceeded its role in making innovations in the construction and application of a provision of the Children Act 1949.

In relation to judicial review proceedings the courts have by contrast on occasion employed the Human Rights Act in a robust way. This was shown for example in *R. (Daly) v Secretary of State for the Home Department* (2001) where the House of Lords held that the courts should adopt a test of proportionality in reviewing executive decisions. Lord Steyn acknowledged the influence of the Human Rights Act firstly in specifying new grounds of review based on violations of convention rights and also by the development of the doctrine of "proportionality" in the sense of the "relative weight accorded to interests and considerations". This did not mean however a consideration of the merits of a decision. This approach may fall short of the expectations of the Strasbourg Court (see *Kingsley v UK* (2001).)

An example of the differing approaches of the domestic and Strasbourg courts is that in regard to the right of prisoners to vote. *R. v Secretary of State for the Home Department Ex p. Pearson and Martinez; Hirst v Attorney-General* (2001) the High Court considered this issue. Article 39 of the First Protocol places a duty on states to hold free elections "under conditions which will ensure the free expression of the opinion of the people in the choice of the legislature." Under s.3 of the Representation of the People Act 1983 convicted prisoners are disenfranchised. Kennedy L.J. found that given the wide margin of appreciation to member states by the case law the exclusion of convicted prisoners from the right to vote was not in violation of the Convention. However, when the case subsequently reached the Strasbourg Court seven judges ruled that the ban violated the Convention. Legislation to change the law is therefore now likely. Kennedy L.J. in his judgment had taken a restrictive view of the role of the courts. He stated that on the question of prisoners' voting rights "there is a broad spectrum of approaches among democratic societies and the United Kingdom falls into the middle of the spectrum." He continued, "In course of time this position may move, either by way of further fine tuning, as was recently done in relation to remand prisoners and others, or more radically, but its position in the spectrum is plainly a matter for parliament not for the courts."

The courts have been generally reluctant to make declarations of incompatibility and even where they have been made they have on occasion been reversed on appeal. For example, in *R. (Alconbury Developments Ltd) v Secretary of State for Transport, the*

Environment and the Regions (2001) the House of Lords, reversing the decision below, held that the Secretary of State's role in planning legislation was not incompatible under Art.6(1) (see also Ch.5).

In *R. (H) v Mental Health Tribunal North and East London Region* (2001) the Court of Appeal held that s.73 of the Mental Health Act 1983 was incompatible with the Convention in placing the burden of proof in satisfying the conditions of discharge of restricted patients on the patients. In response to the decision the Mental Health Act (Remedial) Order was made changing the onus of proof.

In *International Transport Roth GmbH v Secretary of State for the Home Department* (2002) the majority decision of the Court of Appeal was that the scheme adopted under Pt II of the Immigration and Asylum Act 1999, which imposed penalties on those responsible for bringing clandestine entrants to the United Kingdom was incompatible with Art.6. It imposed strict liability on the carriers and also reversed the burden of proof. As a result of the decision new provisions were included in the Immigration, Asylum and Nationality Act, 2002.

In *R. v Secretary of State for Home Department Ex p. (1) Anthony Anderson and (2) John Hope Taylor* (2003), the House of Lords held that the Secretary of State was not entitled, as a member of the executive, to fix the tariff element of mandatory life sentence for murder. It made a declaration that s.29 of the Crime (Sentences) Act 1997 was incompatible with Art.6 of the ECHR. A declaration was also made in *R. (D) v Secretary of State for the Home Department* (2002) by Stanley Burnton J. The case involved a prisoner who had served his tariff under a discretionary life sentence and whose release had been authorised by a mental health tribunal. In such cases it was the practice of the Home Secretary to refer the case to the Parole Board to decide whether the prisoner should be freed. But the minister was under no legal obligation to do so. This was insufficient to satisfy the requirements of Art.5(4), since a person could not be said to have access to a court to test the lawfulness of his detention if such access depended on the approval of a minister.

Thus the domestic courts have shifted between several possible stances in relation to apparent conflict between UK legislation and Convention rights. They may accept that the operation of the current law is within the margin of appreciation accorded to states and leave any change in the status quo to the legislature. This was the minimalist approach taken in relation to prisoners' voting rights and which was evidenced in the analysis of Laws L.J. (dissenting) in *Roth*. He argued that it was misleading to describe Art.6 rights as "absolute" and drew attention to the differing roles which fell properly to the courts on the one hand or to parliament and the executive on the other; he referred to the two latter as "the democratic powers". He noted that "the constitutional responsibility of the democratic powers particularly includes the security of the state's borders thus including immigration control, and that of the courts particularly includes the doing of criminal justice." The question was that if the statute in question was to be treated as an administrative scheme for immigration control then the courts should accord a much greater role to parliament in deciding whether there was a violation of Convention rights than if it was to be regarded as a criminal statute. His approach emphasised that it is for the legislature to effect substantive changes rather than for the judiciary to stretch the statute beyond its limits.

Fast-track procedure

Section 10 and Sch.2 allow for a "fast-track" procedure, by which the executive can act to amend legislation in order to remove incompatibility with the Convention, where a declaration of incompatibility had been made. There is some criticism of this in the sense that it will bypass some parliamentary debate. A similar procedure will be available to implement any legislation arising from an adverse ruling in the Strasbourg Court.

Obligations of public authorities

The Act gives public authorities a special position. Under s.6(1) they must act compatibly with the Convention. Parliamentary supremacy is upheld by s.6(2) of the Human Rights Act. This provides that subs.6(1) does not apply to an act if "(a) as a result of one or more provisions of primary legislation, the authority could not have acted differently; or (b) in the case of one of more provisions of, or made under, primary legislation which is compatible with the Convention rights, the authority was acting so as to give effect to or enforce those provisions." Public authorities include courts and tribunals but not Parliament in its legislative capacity. New causes of action therefore, namely breaches of Convention rights by public authorities, are created by the Act. In addition, the Articles of the Convention included in the Act may be cited as an additional ground of judicial review under the Procedure now set out in the Civil Procedure (Amendment No.4) Rules.

The definition of public authority

The remedies available for a breach of s.6 by a public authority can be sought either by way of judicial review on the basis of illegality or by way of private proceedings in tort for breach of statutory duty. It may also be a defence under some circumstances that an authority is in breach of its s.6 obligations. It is important to distinguish a fully public body from a body whose public character springs only from the fact that its functions are of a public nature. Fully public bodies are directly answerable for failure to adhere to the Convention in all their actions, whereas quasi-public bodies are not to be held liable directly under the Act if they fail to conduct their private functions (such as employment of their staff) in strict accordance with the Convention. Some bodies such as government departments and local authorities, are obviously public bodies for all purposes in connection with the Act. Others may be more difficult to categorise.

Three kinds of public authorities are covered by the Act, namely pure public authorities, court and tribunals and quasi-public authorities of a kind defined in s.6(3)(b), that is "any person certain of whose functions are functions of a public nature". Parliament is excluded. A person is not a public authority by this section if the nature of the act or omission is private. Some bodies are obviously public bodies, including government departments, local authorities, police officers and immigration officials, for example. An instance of a s.6(3)(b) type of body is Railtrack. This is a public authority when it exercises public functions in its role of safety regulator but it also acts privately in its role as a business with duties to its shareholders. Two sources of law are of assistance in determining whether a body is public or private; firstly the European Community Law cases (see *Foster v British Gas* (1990)) and secondly the case law on judicial review (see *R. v Panel on Takeovers and Mergers, Ex p. Datafin* (1987)).

The approach of the courts to the definition of a public authority under the Human Rights Act has been relatively cautious. In an early case to raise this issue the Court of Appeal held that a housing foundation which had closed a care home was not a public authority within the meaning of s.6 of the

Human Rights Act. This was despite the fact that the foundation received public funds and was regulated by the state. In *Donoghue v Poplar Housing and Regeneration Community Association Ltd* (2001) the Court of Appeal gave extensive consideration to the factors which should be taken into account in deciding whether a body is a public body. It was of the view that a local authority in privatizing some functions would not automatically make the actions of the private company public in nature. More controversially it stated that providing houses for rent was not in itself a public duty, no matter which section of society the houses were for. It also stated that the motivation of the organisation was more likely to be in the public good but that was not an indication that it was a public body in terms of s.4 HRA. However, in this borderline case Poplar was functioning as a public body. In *R. v Leonard Cheshire Foundation Ltd* (2002) the Court of Appeal held that the Foundation was not a public authority for the purposes of the Act. This was a controversial decision since the Foundation received public funding, was state regulated and if it had not provided long-stay residential care the state would have been obliged to so so. (See also *R. (Beer) v Hampshire Farmers' Markets Ltd* (2004)). In *Aston Cantlow and Wilmcote with Billesley Parochial Church Council v Wallbank* (2003) the House of Lords, reversing the Court of Appeal decision held that a parochial church council was not a public body. The functions of such councils were primarily concerned with pastoral and administrative matters within the parish and were not wholly of a public nature and so not core public authorities under s.6(1) HRA. The council had therefore no obligation to act compatibly with Convention rights. The Parliamentary Joint Committee on Human Rights endorsed the *Aston Cantlow* approach in a report in April 2004.

An area of controversy is whether public authorities are exercising private law or public law in employment matters. In English law employment law questions, including those in the public sector, are considered private law. On the other hand, in the Strasbourg court employment issues concerning public officials are for the most part regarded as an aspect of public law (see *Balfour v UK* (1997)). (See also p.81).

Standing

The Act can only be used to bring proceedings by a person who is or would be a victim of the violation of the Convention (s.7).

This is a much narrower definition of standing than that employed for judicial review proceedings. This means that proceedings under the Act can only be brought by a person who would have had the standing to take his or her case to the Strasbourg court, that is someone actually and directly affected or at risk of being affected by the act or omission complained of. This is a narrower set of potential litigants than would be regarded as having the standing to bring ordinary judicial review proceedings and does not include local authorities. Any interest group wishing to enforce convention rights will need to find a "victim" to act as applicant.

The restriction puts a brake on the possibility of "public interest" litigation in the human rights field. Thus, pressure groups may not be included, unlike the position for judicial review (see for example *R. v Lord Chancellor, Ex p. Child Poverty Action Group* (1998)). On the other hand, the European Court of Human Rights has accepted as victims those who were potential victims. Thus for example a homosexual man was a victim where the existence of legislation criminalising homosexuality affected his private life even though there had been no actual or threatened prosecution (*Norris v Ireland* (1988)). This broad view was applied by the Administrative Court in the case of Diane Pretty where it took the view that a refusal by the Attorney-General to give an undertaking not to prosecute should her husband assist her suicide might constitute a cause of action for an ECHR challenge and granted permission to proceed with the action (see p.67). However a more restrictive view was adopted in the House of Lords.

In *Rusbridger v The Attorney-General* (2003), the House held that a claim for a declaration as to the meaning of s.3 Treason Felony Act 1848 or for a declaration of incompatibility under the Human Rights Act 1998 was unnecessary and should be dismissed. The applicants had appealed against the Administrative Court's refusal of permission to apply for judicial review of the Attorney-General's refusal to state whether or not a prosecution would be brought under s.3 if the applicants published a series of articles supporting the abolition of the monarchy and the establishment of a republic. They had presented a different argument before the Court of Appeal, abandoning the claim about the Attorney-General's action or inaction and seeking a declaration about the meaning of an Act of Parliament and a declaration of incompatibility if appropriate. The Court of Appeal allowed the applicants to proceed and the Attorney-General appealed. The House of

Lords held that the litigation was unnecessary and the application was dismissed. It was clear that no-one who advocated the abolition of the monarchy by peaceful and constitutional means was at any risk of prosecution. Lord Rodger in the judgment pointed out that the applicants were unaffected either in their actions or wellbeing by the 1848 Act and were not "victims".

Time limits

The Act creates positive causes of action for acts or omissions which took place after October 2, 2000 but it can provide a defence to proceedings brought by the public authority whenever the act or omission took place. There is also a limitation period for acts against public authorities of one year from the date that the act complained of took place. This can, however, be extended when the court considers it equitable in all the circumstances. This one-year time limit only applies to claims which directly allege breach of a Convention right by a public authority. A claim form in judicial review proceedings must be filed promptly and in any event not later than three months after the grounds for making the claim first arose. The time limit cannot be extended by agreement between the parties.

Procedure and Remedies

The Act does not set up any special courts for resolution of claims. Argument derived from the Convention may be made in every public forum in which legal rights are determined, from an employment tribunal to the House of Lords.

Which court?

The appropriate court for a claim under the Human Rights Act 1998 will depend on the subject matter of the complaint and the remedy sought. The normal rules apply, except that a claim that a court as a public authority under s.7(1)(a) of the 1998 Act has violated the Convention can only be commenced in the High Court and must be tried by a High Court, Crown Court or County Court judge, not by a deputy, a master or a recorder. A claim for a declaration of incompatibility cannot be made in the County Court, nor can it be tried by a deputy High Court judge, a Master or a district judge.

Cases brought by way of judicial review are dealt with by the Administrative Court (formerly the Crown Office List). In the new Civil Procedure Rules, Pt 54, a claim for judicial review is defined as "a claim to review the lawfulness of: (i) an enactment; or (ii) a decision, action or failure to act in relation to the exercise of a public function". The prerogative orders have been renamed, with mandamus becoming "a mandatory order", certiorari "a quashing order" and prohibition "a prohibiting order". Judicial review procedure must be used in seeking any of these orders, or in seeking an injunction to restrain a person from acting in any office or employment in which he is not entitled to act. If the application concerns a human rights issue the claim form must indicate that. It should also give precise details of the Convention right alleged to have been infringed, the form of infringement and the relief sought. These details include any request for a declaration of incompatibility, full details of the legislative provision said to be incompatible and any claim for damages in respect of a judicial act.

Remedies

Section 8(1) of the Act authorises a court which has found that an act or proposed act of a public authority is unlawful, to grant "such relief or remedy or make such order within its power as it considers just and appropriate". These remedies will include damages, declarations, injunctions and relief available by way of judicial review. Courts must take into account, when deciding whether to award damages, the principles applied by the European Court of Human Rights in relation to award of compensation. In fact the compensation awards made by Strasbourg are usually quite low, between £10,000 and £15,000 (see, for example, *Johnson v UK* (1997)). It should be noted however that the Strasbourg Court has consistently recognised what is known in civil law systems as "moral damage", which includes issues of personal integrity, and has awarded damages for emotional distress and loss of opportunity for psychological or social benefits. For example, in a series of cases against the UK it found violations in the arrangements for taking children into care against their parents' wishes and in the absence of remedies and length of judicial proceedings when redress was sought.

Section 11 of the Act provides that a person may rely on a Convention right without prejudice to any other right or freedom conferred on him or her by or under any (other) law having effect in the UK. One safeguard in the Act is that it is not generally possible to make a claim for damages against a court which has breached the Convention, even though it is a public authority. Section 9 requires proceedings relating to an unlawful act of a first instance court to be brought on appeal from the decision or by way of judicial review. In addition there is no remedy in damages where the breach is caused by Act of Parliament.

Retrospectivity

How far does the Human Rights Act 1998 apply to disputes which arose before the Act came into force? This issue has arisen in several cases and is the subject of academic dispute. The House of Lords considered the issue in *Wilson v First County Trust Ltd (No.2)* (2003) which was an appeal by the Secretary of State for Trade and Industry from a decision of the Court of Appeal declaring s.127(3) of the Consumer Credit Act 1974 to be incompatible with a pawnbroker's human rights. Mrs Wilson had pawned her BMW, and when the pawnbroker sought repayment of his loan, she claimed their agreement was unenforceable because it did not contain all the terms required by the 1974 Act. Section 127(3) barred the court from making an enforcement order in the absence of a document containing all the prescribed terms of the loan agreement. The Secretary of State argued that the Human Rights Act did not apply to an agreement made before October 2000 when the Act came into force. The House of Lords agreed: there was a presumption against the retrospective application of legislation. Its basis was that parliament could not have intended to alter the law applying to past events and transactions in such a way as to change people's rights of obligations unfairly. There was no explicit provision in the 1998 Act to make it operate retrospectively. Section 3(1) of the 1998 Act, which provides: "So far as it is possible to do so, primary legislation and subordinate legislation must be read and given effect in a way which is compatible with the Convention rights", was not intended to alter the existing rights and obligations of the parties to an agreement made before the 1998 Act came into force. So the Human Rights Act was not available to the parties in the case as an aid to interpreting s.127(3).

In a controversial decision the House of Lords considered the effect of s.22(4) of the Human Rights Act. This provides a remedy for the victim of an unlawful act is available in proceedings brought by or at the instigation of a public authority whenever the act in question took place; but otherwise does not apply to an act taking place before October 2000. The decision in *Wilson* has been forcefully challenged by some academic commentators. In *R. v Lambert* (2001), the House of Lords considered the question whether an accused person could rely on a breach of Convention rights by the police or prosecution in an appeal against a decision made before the coming into force of the Human Rights Act.

The House held that the Human Rights Act provisions were not intended to apply to events before the date they came into force. Accordingly, a defendant whose trial took place before the coming into force of s.7(1)(b) of the Human Rights Act 1998 was not entitled, after its coming into force, to rely in an appeal on an alleged breach of his Convention rights under s.22(4) of that Act.

Court decisions made before that date were not to be impugned under s.6 on the ground that the court or tribunal had acted in a way incompatible with Convention rights. Lord Steyn, dissenting, expressed the view that: "It will be noted that the effect of s.6(1) is to provide that it *is unlawful* for the House *to act* in a way which is incompatible with a Convention right. The question is whether this provision applies to the appeal before the House. Given that it is expressed to limit the way in which a appellate court may act incompatibly with a Convention right. Surely, for an appellate court to uphold a conviction obtained in breach of a Convention right must be *to act* incompatibly with a Convention right. It is unlawful for it to do so. So interpreted no true retrospectivity is involved."

In *Kansal v United Kingdom* Application no. 21413/02 (2004), the Strasbourg court upheld an appeal against by a pharmacist convicted of mortgage fraud in 1992. At the applicant's trial significant use was made of statements made under compulsion at his bankruptcy hearing. The House of Lords had held (*R. v Kansal* (2001)) that he could not benefit from the 1998 Act because it was bound by *Lambert* to hold that the Act could not be applied retrospectively in criminal appeals. The Strasbourg decision puts in doubt the current English law position that convictions made before the Human Rights Act came into force cannot be appealed on the basis of violations of rights under the Act. An application of the principle is to be seen in *R. v Lyons* (2003). Lyons had been convicted of offences of dishonesty in relation to a City takeover. The prosecution had relied on admissions Lyons had been compelled to make to Department of Trade investigators. The European Court of Human Rights subsequently found that the use of the admissions had infringed his right to a fair trial. On the strength of this decision, Lyons appealed but the Appeal Court dismissed his appeal. The House of Lords also dismissed his appeal, holding that the Court of Appeal was bound to accept the substantive law as it stood at the time of the trial. The Human Rights Act 1998 did not apply retrospectively (*Lambert*). English courts were not obliged to follow the judgment of the European Court of Human Rights, since UK treaty obligations which might bind the United Kingdom, were not directly binding on the domestic courts.

In *Matthews v Ministry of Defence* (2003), a former serviceman suffering from asbestos-related disease claimed damages for personal injury. His claim was denied under s.10 of the Crown Proceedings Act 1947, which specifically excludes tort claims by members of the armed forces. The judge at first instance held s.10 to be incompatible with the fair trial provisions of the European Human Rights convention. The House of Lords, however, held that the fair trial rights under Art.6(1) applied only to civil rights which could, on arguable grounds, be recognised under domestic law and where the restriction on the right of access to the courts was procedural in nature. The bar on servicemen suing the Ministry had long applied at common law in addition to statute. The government had provided a system of no-fault compensation for injured servicemen so that the bar was not procedural only but a matter of substantive law.

In Re McKerr (AP) (2004) concerned a victim of a shoot-to-kill incident by the Royal Ulster Constabulary in Northern Ireland. The claimant's father was killed in 1982, and after a lengthy odyssey his son obtained a favourable ruling from the Strasbourg court, which awarded damages for the authorities' failure to hold an effective investigation, in violation of Art.2. The court awarded compensation, which was paid to the claimant by the British government, but there were no plans to reopen the investigation. The claimant sought judicial review of this failure, and the case ended up in the House of Lords. The fatal flaw in the case, the House held, was that the death had occurred before the coming into force of the Act, which placed it outside the reach of Art.6. Parliament could not have intended the Human Rights Act to apply differently to the primary obligation, *i.e.* to protect life and a consequential obligation, to investigate a death. The decision is notable for dicta of Lord Hoffmann, rejecting the idea that Art.2 embodied a broad common law principle: "The common law develops from case to case in harmony with statute. Its principles are generalizations from detailed rules, not abstract propositions from which those rules are deduced."

Effect of Human Rights Act on private law

The potential horizontal effect of the Act has been hotly disputed. Sir Richard Buxton has argued that it cannot have a horizontal effect, while Sir William Wade maintains that it can. At the minimum however, the Act has an indirect effect on private law, that is on the legal relations between private juristic persons.

Though the Human Rights Act is directed entirely at public authorities, its provisions may well have an indirect impact on disputes between private individuals. Private individuals cannot sue one another for breach of Convention rights, but the Act does create an obligation on the courts, as public bodies, to protect individuals from violations of their rights by other private individuals. This obligation arises where the courts are not otherwise bound by statute or precedent. Where the court has a discretion to interpret a statutory provision, for example in a matter of family law, a common law right, it will be obliged to do so in accordance with the Convention. The areas in which the Act impacts on private law are as follows:

(a) Interpreting legislation In the first place, while the Act makes no mention of any form of horizontal effect under the Convention, it appears clear that s.3, requiring legislation to be interpreted in a way which is compatible with Convention rights, applies to all legislation whether public or private in nature. This is a broad obligation which transcends the narrow requirements of legalistic interpretation where Convention rights are at issue. The Privy Council has held in a number of Commonwealth cases that constitutional provisions must be read so as to give individuals the full extent of such rights. In *Ministry of Home Affairs v Fisher* (A.C. 1980), for example, the court refused to apply to an article of the Bermuda constitution a rule of statutory interpretation normally applied to Acts of Parliament, which would have required "child" to be read as meaning legitimate child. But it remains to be seen whether the English courts will treat the Convention as a constitutional provision in the full sense. Section 3 will apply in all cases where a Convention right is at issue.

The impact on the way in which statute is interpreted is likely in the long run to be considerable, at least in areas where Convention rights are important. Where they are, the Act will bring about a shift of approach which will entrench a human rights "culture" to an extent not previously experienced. An analogous approach is already required in relation to European Union law, so the courts are already accustomed to interpretative obligations imposed by statute.

(b) Courts as public authorities In addition some measure of horizontal effect arises because courts and tribunals are public authorities for the purposes of the Act and are themselves bound to give effect to Convention standards in giving judgment even in cases involving only private individuals. The difficulty in this is, however, that the litigant has to have a cause of action in private law to get his case to court in the first place. Thus, for example, a litigant could not simply go to court against a national newspaper stating that it has violated her rights to privacy under Art.8. A national newspaper is not a public authority and the Act is not therefore binding on it. The only workable option for the claimant would be to proceed directly against the newspaper using some existing cause of action such as trespass or breach of confidence and then argue that the court's duty to act compatibly with the Convention (balancing the right to privacy under Art.8 with the freedom of expression under Art.10) requires it to act for the claimant.

However, since the Convention rights are not specifically incorporated into English law they can only be utilised as principles and values rather than clear entitlements. One problem is that although courts are included as public authorities there is no direct sanction for their failure to observe a Convention right. Section 9 provides that "proceedings" may only be brought in respect of a judicial violation of s.6 by way of appeal, judicial review or in such other forum as may be prescribed by rules. However, s.9(2) provides that this does not affect any rule of law which prevents a court from being the subject of judicial review. It thus preserves the common law rule precluding judicial review of High Court decisions for jurisdictional error (*Re Racal Communications Ltd* (1981)).

(c) Interpreting the common law Section 2 of the Act requires that a court or tribunal determining a question which has arisen in connection with a Convention right, should take into account decisions of the European Court of Human Rights and the Commission. It is important to note that the Act itself makes no mention of the common law, unlike the Canadian and

South African constitutions which explicitly apply constitutional rights to common law. In the case of Canada the Bill of Rights specifically states that "any law that is inconsistent with the provisions of the Constitution is to the extent of the inconsistency of no force or effect" (Constitution Act 1982, s.52). However, Home Secretary Jack Straw stressed in the Parliamentary debates, "the Convention . . . is not there to deal with abuses of rights by persons acting in a private capacity" (*Hansard*, H.C. vol. 37, col. 1341). At common law the English courts have previously held that they can pay attention to the requirements of the Convention when exercising judicial discretion in a private law context (see *Middlebrook Mushrooms v Transport and General Workers Union* (1993) and *Rantzen v Mirror Group Newspapers (1986) Ltd* (1994)).

Strasbourg decisions and private law

In practice the Strasbourg court itself has been reluctant to intervene in private law matters. One example was *Young, James and Webster* (1981), where it was found that the enforcement in private law that of closed shop agreement violated Art.11's guarantee of freedom of association. However, in a number of other cases involving Arts 8–11 particularly, the court has not found a duty of positive obligation on the part of the state and left the substantive content of the Article in question to the state's discretion. For example, in *Earl Spencer and Countess Spencer v UK* (1998) it found that a claim that the UK government had failed to protect the Earl from invasion of privacy was ill founded. However, it "would not exclude" the possibility that the lack of a remedy for such violations could infringe Art.8. The UK courts will not be able to draw on extensive existing jurisprudence about the application of the Convention in private law. It could in any case be argued that the Convention should only have vertical effect because the state is the body posing the main risk to rights. In general it has far more resources to interfere with individual rights. Undoubtedly, the general increase in debate and concern about human rights will eventually have the effect of filtering such matters into all areas of law.

Privacy

The shape of the English law of privacy has been clarified (or clouded, according to some) by litigation since the coming into force of the Human Rights Act. Lord Justice Sedley in the Court of Appeal, ruling on a preliminary issue in *Douglas v Hello* (2001), appeared to suggest the Act could be used to underpin a freestanding right of privacy, since in his view the law no longer required an artificial relationship of confidentiality between the party whose privacy was invaded and the invader. But the judiciary as a whole has so far been reluctant to take the law in this direction, though recent cases have expanded the area of privacy somewhat. Contrast the attitude of the Strasbourg court, which in *Peck v United Kingdom* (2003) recently criticised the inaction of the English judiciary. In a recent English authority, *Wainwright v Home Office* (2003), the House of Lords decided there was no tort of invasion of privacy. The claimant and her son were strip searched when they visited another son in prison. They argued that the prison officers were liable for invasion of privacy, contrary to Art.8 of the European Convention. The Lords held that although privacy was a value underlying the law of breach of confidence, it was not in itself a principle of law and there was no tort of invasion of privacy. Article 8 did not require English law to develop such a tort. Lord Hoffmann's speech, which is short by modern standards, was approved by the other law lords. He highlighted the difficulties of bringing a tort of privacy into being. In the United States, privacy had generated four different types of interference with a person's "right to be let alone". He cited with approval dicta of Sir Robert Megarry in *Malone v Metropolitan Police Commissioner* (1979): "Where parliament has refrained from legislating on a point which is plainly suitable for legislation, it is indeed difficult for the court to lay down new rules of common law or equity that will carry out the Crown's treaty obligations, or to discover for the first time that such rules have always existed." Lord Justice Sedley in *Douglas* was doing no more than suggesting that the existing tort of confidentiality might reasonably now be relabeled breach of privacy. It was important to distinguish between privacy as a value underlying the existence of a legal rule, and privacy as a principle of law itself.

In *Peck v United Kingdom* the claimant had been captured on closed circuit television attempting suicide by slashing his wrists in the high street. The images had been used in a campaign to show the benefits of closed circuit TV. The disclosure had been a disproportionate interference with P's private life and accordingly infringed his rights under Art.8. His rights under Art.13 had also been violated, since the English courts provided him with no effective remedy for the breach of his Art.8 right. In *Perry v United*

Kingdom (2003) the applicant's Art.8 rights were infringed when police covertly took video pictures of him in the police station and subsequently used them in an identification procedure. The procedure adopted by the police did not comply with the codes of practice under the Police and Criminal Evidence Act 1984, s.66. Privacy hit the headlines again in *Campbell v Mirror Group Newspapers* (2004), a case which concerned a newspaper's rebuttal of lies told by a supermodel who denied that she was a drug addict. The newspaper published an article establishing that she had attended meetings of Narcotics Anonymous, together with a photograph of her leaving an NA session. The House of Lords, by a majority of three to two, held that publication of the picture (though not the accompanying text) violated her privacy rights. The decision seems to be confined to its own facts and is difficult to justify in principle. Lord Hoffmann, who was in the minority, said: " . . . the differences of opinion relate to a very narrow point which arises on the unusual facts of this case . . . But the importance of this case lies in the statements of general principle on the way in which the law should strike a balance between the right to privacy and the right to freedom of expression, on which the House is unanimous." Lord Nicholls defined the modern tort as the misuse of private information. The touchstone of private life was essentially whether in respect of the disclosed facts the person in question had a reasonable expectation of privacy. He doubted whether, given her previous public lies, the model could reasonably expect the newspaper to refrain from publicising her attendance at NA meetings. For the majority, Lady Hale said the picture had enhanced the model's sense of being followed or betrayed and because it might interfere with her treatment for addiction was a violation of her privacy rights. For the minority, Lord Hoffmann said succinctly: "Judges are not newspaper editors . . . it would be inconsistent with the approach that has been taken in a number of recent landmark cases for a newspaper to be held strictly liable for exceeding what a judge considers to have been necessary." However, the *Campbell* case is not the first time the idea that a photograph may be more objectionable than a written account has been enunciated. Waller LJ in *D v L* (2003) summarising existing authorities, stressed: "A photograph is more than the information you get from it. A Court may restrain the publication of an improperly obtained photograph even if the taker is free to describe the information which the photograph provides or even if the information revealed by the photograph is in the public domain."

Striking a balance between Art.8 and Art.10 rights is likely to continue to cause problems for the courts. An earlier case which also dealt with privacy issues was *Venables v News Group Newspapers Ltd* (2001), which concerned the killers of the toddler Jamie Bulger. Granting them a continuing injunction against publication of their whereabouts on release from prison, Butler-Sloss L.J. said the law of confidentiality could extend to cover information about people's whereabouts where publication might put their lives at risk. The injunctions were necessary to protect the applicants against the "real and strong possibility" of physical harm or death.

Supervision

The Act was heavily criticised for its failure to set up a Human Rights Commission. Such a body could have assumed responsibility for supervising the implementation of the Act. As it is, it is left to the courts to carry out this task for which the judiciary have undergone special training. By contrast, in Northern Ireland and in Scotland a newly established human rights commission oversees the adequacy of the protection of human rights. However, a Joint Parliamentary Committee has been established to oversee the implementation of the Act.

In its Sixth Report of Session 2002–2003 it stated that there was a compelling case for setting up a Human Rights Commission. In May 2004 the government announced plans to create a single all-powerful commission to fight all forms of discrimination The new body, the Equality and Human Rights Commission, will replace three existing commissions—for racial equality, disability rights, and equal opportunities. It will also oversee laws to stamp out ageism and discrimination over religion or sexual orientation.

Preliminary assessment

Four years after the coming into force of the Human Rights Act, a fairly clear picture is emerging of the impact of this legislation. It is important to bear in mind that the Act did not emerge out of the blue: The rights it embeds in English law were there before it came into force, but where they were not available by statute or at common law had to be pursued all the way to Strasbourg. And one should not underestimate the extent to which European human rights standards had been colouring the decisions of English judges in the years before the Act became law. Judicial review of administrative action was an expanding field well before the millennium and one can view the Act as a further step down an already well paved road. Nonetheless, it has produced significant cultural changes in English law, not least the rise of a flourishing caste of self-proclaimed human rights lawyers.

Lord Lester Q.C., one of the Act's main architects, regards it as remarkable that the Act happened at all, attributing it to a brief period of glasnost at the start of the Tony Blair government, and siting it among that government's constitution reforms, including devolution, freedom of information and reform of the House of Lords. In a recent lecture to the Bar Council's law reform committee, he warned: "There is always a risk, even in countries with entrenched written constitutional chargers of fundamental rights of future emasculation or worse. In the case of the Human Rights Act that risk is both increased by the relative ease with which the executive can persuade an executive-controlled House of Commons to pass legislation, yet also diminished by the fact that the Convention rights contained in the act are internationally protected by the two European Courts. We should not place too much faith in supra-national legal mechanisms to deter a future government hell-bent on weakening or destroying the Human Rights Act. The best safeguard is surely the nurturing of a deep-seated culture of respect for human rights among governors and governed."

The government's discomfort at the application of Convention standards by the courts has been articulated most strongly by the Home Secretary. When the special immigration appeals commission granted bail with stringent to an Algerian national, G, who had become mentally ill while held without trial in Belmarsh top security prison on suspicion of links to Al-Qaeda, the Home Secretary described the decision as "bonkers". He was equally robust about an earlier decision of Collins J., *R. (Q) v Secretary of State for the Home Department* (2003), affirmed by the Court of Appeal the same year. The case concerned the denial of asylum support to applicants who failed to apply for asylum at the earliest practicable moment after their arrival in the UK. The judge held that the procedure imposed by s. 55 of the Nationality, Immigration and Asylum Act 2002 was unfair to the applicants since it left no room for the examination of their individual circumstances. The Home Secretary responded: "Frankly I am personally fed up with having to deal with situation where parliament debates issues and the judges then overthrow them." Clearly the Act retains its controversial status.

The potential for friction between an aggressively populist executive and a judiciary basing itself on human rights principles is by no means exhausted. Principle requires that the judiciary should not bow to public opinion where basic rights are concerned. As Chaskalson P. put it in the landmark South African case which abolished the death penalty: "The very reason for establishing the new legal order, and for vesting the power of judicial review of all legislation in the courts, was to protect the rights of minorities and others who cannot protect their rights adequately through the democratic process. Those who are entitled to claim this protection include the social outcasts and marginalised people of our society."

4. KILLING, TORTURE AND SLAVERY

Articles 2, 3 and 4 protect the most fundamental rights: those to physical security and protection from ill treatment. In *McCann v UK* (1995) the court stated that Art.2 "ranks as one of the most fundamental provisions in the Convention" and that "together with Art.3, it enshrines one of the basic values of the democratic societies making up the Council of Europe".

THE RIGHT TO LIFE

Article 2 of the European Convention requires that everyone's right to life shall be protected by law. In peacetime derogation from Art.2 is not allowed. The Article does not, however, stretch to giving unconditional protection for life itself nor does it have any bearing on the quality of life. The purpose is to protect the individual from arbitrary deprivation of life by state authorities and to place some responsibility on the state in the case of unlawful killings. (See also death penalty p.19).

Duties of the State

To safeguard life

The state has a positive duty to protect life. This does not mean, however, that it must eschew allowing the taking of medical risks for the general good. In *Association X v UK* (1978) an association of parents whose children had suffered damage or death as a result of vaccination claimed that the state had violated Art.2 since the vaccination programme was government-sponsored. The Commission disagreed, stating that "there exists a general common knowledge that vaccination schemes involve certain risks". The system of control and supervision established by the state was sufficient.

By contrast, in *Edwards v UK* (2002) the court found that putting a prisoner in a cell with an individual who had a history of violence, without sufficient precautions was a breach of the state's obligation to protect life. There was a violation of Art.2.

Lifesaving medical treatment

However, the Commission also stated in *A v UK* that "the concept that everyone's life shall be protected by law enjoins the state not only to refrain from taking life intentionally, but, further, to take appropriate steps to safeguard life". It is at least arguable therefore, that the state may have a duty to provide the medical treatment necessary to preserve life. In *R. v Cambridgeshire Health Authority, Ex p. B* (1995) the Court of Appeal, quashing the High Court decision, held that the health authority was entitled to refuse to fund potential lifesaving treatment for a young child since it was entitled to deploy its resources as best it could. Will such a decision need to be revisited in the light of the Human Rights Act? No clear answer is given in *Taylor v UK* (1994), where the Commission considered a complaint by the parents of children killed or injured by nurse Beverley Allitt. The parents argued that financial and other shortcomings of the health service had allowed an untrained, dangerous individual to care for their children unsupervised. The Commission held that the organisation and funding of the National Health Service did not fall within the scope of Art.2:

> "Any doubts which may consequently arise as to the policies adopted in the field of public health are, in the Commission's opinion, matters for public and political debate which fall outside the scope of Article 2 and the other provisions of the Convention".

It is open to argument, for example, that even if a reasonable allocation of health care resources was not a breach of Art.2,

Art.14 requires that public authorities safeguard Convention rights without discrimination on any ground. It might therefore be that if lifesaving treatment was withheld on grounds of age, or youth, or mental condition, such action was a breach of Art.14 taken together with Art.2.

Reasonableness test

It appears that a body will be in breach of Art.2 if it fails to act reasonably in defence of life. *In Guerra v Italy* (1998) however, the Court held that the authorities only had an obligation to inform local people about environmental dangers which posed a potential threat to health in "circumstances which foreseeably and on substantial grounds present a real risk of danger". That was not so in that case.

The authorities might therefore be able to argue in defence of an act under Art.2 that they had acted reasonably. The common law has accepted the justification of the interests of the patient for the decision of doctors to turn off the life-support system of someone who is in a permanent vegetative state. In *Airedale NHS Trust v Bland* (1993) Lord Mustill had considered the argument of the best interests of the community but though this was persuasive "in social terms", did not consider the House of Lords was qualified to make such an assessment. The court found there was no violation of Art.2 in a case involving the suicide of a mentally ill prisoner. On the whole, the authorities made a reasonable response to his conduct and had not omitted any step which should reasonably have been taken (*Keenan v UK* (2001)).

Absolutely necessary force

There are three exceptions to the prohibition on taking life by force. These are the defence of any person from unlawful violence, effecting a lawful arrest or preventing the escape of a detainee and quelling a riot or insurrection. The force used must be "no more than absolutely necessary". In *McCann and Others v UK* (1994), three IRA members were in Gibraltar to plant a car bomb. While they were preparing to do so, they were shot dead by soldiers in the street. The soldiers claimed in each case that they had opened fire because they suspected that their targets were about to set off a bomb by remote control. None of the three were armed or carrying any remote control device. The bomb they were planning to plant was later found across the border in Spain. A coroner's jury in Gibraltar found the killings lawful. Attempts by the families to bring judicial review proceedings were dismissed.

The court held that in assessing whether the use of force had been absolutely necessary it must subject the deprivation of life to the most careful scrutiny and take into account not only the actions of the state agents who used the force, but all the surrounding circumstances. The test of "absolutely necessary" requires that "a stricter and more compelling test of necessity must be employed from that normally applicable when determining whether the state's action is 'necessary in a democratic society'". The court decided that the actions of the soldiers who shot the terrorists was not in violation of Art.2 but there was a violation as regards the control and organisation of the operation. They refused however to award damages, accepting that the terrorists had been intending to plant a bomb. The test for "absolutely necessary" force was also elaborated in *Stewart v UK* (1984), arising from the accidental killing of a 13-year-old boy by a soldier firing a plastic bullet into a rioting crowd. The Commission held this was not a violation of Art.2. Force was "absolutely necessary" if it was "strictly proportionate to the achievement of the permitted purpose". It also held that Art.2(2) covered unintentional killings as well as intentional. The test applied by the Court and Commission imposes a higher standard than that under English statutory law, where a subjective test of reasonableness is applied (Criminal Law Act 1967, s.3).

Procedural requirements

The Article requires proper investigation of suspicious deaths (see *McCann v UK* (1994); *Yasa v Turkey* (1999)). Here the procedure for inquests and police investigation have come under scrutiny. In *Taylor v UK* (1994) the parents failed in a claim that failure to establish a public inquiry into the killings breached Art.2. In *Jordan v UK* (2001) the Court found a breach of procedure under Art.2.

As a result of these decisions a number of English cases have considered the procedure for coroners' inquests. In *R. (Middleton) v HM Coroner for the Western District of Somerset and Avon* (2004) the House of Lords set out the conditions which should apply when the death was the result of an act or omission of agents of the state. In particular these specify the need for a broader remit for jury verdicts.

Abortion

An interesting question is whether an unborn child has the right to life under Art.2. Unlike Art.4 of the American Convention on Human Rights, Art.2 does not declare that life starts at conception. In *Paton v UK* (1980), the Commission ruled that the abortion of a ten-week-old foetus to protect the physical or mental health of a pregnant woman was not a breach of Art.2. The issue of whether a foetus has a right to life was considered in *Open Door Counselling and Dublin Well Woman v Ireland* (1992). The case concerned the applicant's rights to disseminate information about abortion rather than the right to abortion. However the Commission did state that Art.2 could restrict the availability of an abortion but it gives no clear guidance on the point. It stated: "National authorities enjoy a wide margin of appreciation in matters of morals, particularly in an area such as the present which touches on matters of belief concerning the nature of human life".

Euthanasia

Passive euthanasia was considered by the Commission in *Wider v Switzerland* (1993), where it held that Art.2 did not require states to make passive euthanasia a crime. There is no authority on active euthanasia.

In *R. v DPP Ex p. Pretty* (2002) the House of Lords held that although certain articles in the Convention conferred on a person a negative right to not to do something such an interpretation did not apply to Art.2. In addition the burden of proof fell on the complainant to show that the DPP's refusal to give an undertaking that her husband would not be prosecuted under s.2(1) of the Suicide Act if he assisted her in taking her life. In addition the argument that she had a right to die was inconsistent with the common law position that someone else cannot take a person's life. It was held that there was no breach of Art.3 since the obligation on the state was not absolute and unqualified. An application to the European Court of Human Rights failed. In *Pretty v United Kingdom* (2002) the European Court of Human Rights held that the right to life under Art.2 did not guarantee the right of self-determination so as to allow a person the right to die.

PROHIBITION ON TORTURE AND INHUMAN/DEGRADING TREATMENT

Article 3 provides that "no one shall be subjected to torture or to inhuman or degrading treatment or punishment." Peacetime derogation is not possible.

Severity of conduct

In two inter-state cases the three levels of conduct were described by the Commission in the *Greek Case* (1969) and by the court in *Ireland v UK* (1978). In the latter these were set as:

(a) Torture: deliberate inhuman treatment causing very serious and cruel suffering;
(b) Inhuman treatment or punishment: the infliction of intense physical and mental suffering;
(c) Degrading treatment: ill-treatment designed to arouse in victims feelings of fear, anguish and inferiority capable of humiliating and debasing them and possibly breaking their physical or moral resistance.

The court also listed factors to take into account, which included sex, age, and state of health of the victim. It stated that the authority's activities should reach a minimum level of severity to bring them within the Article. "Degrading" did not mean simply disagreeable or uncomfortable. Actions in private as well as in front of others can fall within the Article.

Torture

The torture threshold was found to have been established in *Aksoy v Turkey* (1997), where the applicant was stripped naked, with his arms tied behind his back, and suspended by his arms. It was significant that this treatment was administered with the aim of obtaining admissions or information from the applicant. In *Denmark v Greece* (1969), the Athens security police were found to have used a system of torture and ill treatment of detainees. This included "the infliction of mental suffering by creating a state of anguish and stress by means other than bodily assault". The Commission's finding of torture was confirmed by the Council of Ministers.

Duty to prevent Torture

The Article imposes a positive obligation on states to prevent torture. In *Chahal v UK* (1997), the court held that deportation of a person to a country where he would face a real risk of torture offended Art.3. There was also a violation in *D v UK* (1997), where the would-be deportee had AIDS. He would have neither emotional nor financial support in the receiving country where there was a poor quality of medical care.

Extradition

In *Soering v UK* (1989), a German national faced extradition from Britain to face capital charges in the United States. He claimed a violation of Art.3, and the court agreed. It took the view that although the death penalty in the United States was not in itself illegal, the fact that the applicant might well be held for years on death row pending execution was a violation for which the UK would be responsible if extradition went ahead.

Inhuman treatment/punishment

Treatment or punishment is inhuman within the meaning of Art.3 if it causes "intense physical or mental suffering" (*Ireland v UK* (1979)). Detainees in Northern Ireland were obliged to stand against a wall for hours. They were interrogated wearing a dark hood and deprived of sleep and adequate food and drink. They were also subjected to noise. The Commission found these techniques to be torture, but the court found them to be inhuman and degrading treatment. The distinction between torture and inhuman treatment is a matter of degree. The threat of torture, if "sufficiently real and imminent", can constitute inhuman treatment as can the infliction of psychological harm. In *X and Y v Netherlands* (1986), the Commission stated that "mental suffering leading to acute psychiatric disturbances falls into the category of treatment prohibited by Art.3 of the Convention".

The applicant in *Ribitsch v Austria* (1995) had been physically abused by the Vienna police. He claimed he had been punched in the head, kidneys and arm and also kicked in the kidneys. He had been pulled to the ground by his hair and his head was banged on the floor. In the view of the court this amounted to inhuman and degrading treatment. Inhuman treatment was also found in *Cyprus v Turkey* (1976), where the state was held responsible for rapes committed by its soldiers. Satisfactory measures were not in place to prevent the attacks and the perpetrators had been inadequately disciplined. The court said that where a person was deprived of his liberty "any recourse to physical force what has not been made strictly necessary by his own conduct diminishes human dignity" and could violate Art.3. The court has declared that the UK has also violated Art.3 in the treatment in prison of a man who was a known suicide risk. Lack of adequate specialist medical supervision before his death combined with additional internal disciplinary punishment on him amounted to inhuman and degrading treatment (*Keenan v UK* (2001)).

There have been a number of decisions concerning Art.3 since the Human Rights Act came into force. In *R. v Offen* (2001) the Court of Appeal held that imposing an automatic life sentence where the prisoner posed no significant risk to the public could amount to inhuman and degrading treatment. Article 3 has also been cited in cases involving asylum seekers. In *R. (Q and Others) v Secretary of State for the Home Department* (2003) the Court of Appeal held that to withdraw financial support for destitute asylum seekers would be a violation of Art.3 if there was a real risk that injury to health would arise. Only those who had applied "as soon as reasonably practicable" after arriving in Britain were eligible for state support. This had been interpreted to mean within three days. However, Arts 3 and 8 were not breached and once the deficiencies in procedure were remedied the policy could proceed. This decision was followed by *Secretary of State for the Home Department v Limbuela* (2004). The Court of Appeal held (Laws L.J. dissenting) that there was no reason to interfere with Administrative Court decisions that the Home Secretary should have provided three asylum seekers with asylum support under the Nationality, Immigration and Asylum Act s.55 to avoid a breach of Art.3. Subsequently the Home Office issued a staff instruction saying that asylum seekers should not be refused state benefits unless it was clear that have some alternative means of support.

Degrading treatment/punishment

Treatment or punishment is degrading if it arouses in the victim
a feeling of fear, anguish and inferiority, capable of humiliating
the victim and possibly breaking his physical or moral resistance.
But conditions have to be very poor to trigger the Article. In
Delazarus v UK (1993) a prisoner was segregated for over four
months as a disciplinary measure. He was not allowed to
communicate or associate with other prisoners and locked in a
cockroach infested cell for 23 hours a day with two half-hour
breaks in a pen the size of a tennis court. The application was
held inadmissible.

A severely disabled person's detention in police custody where
provisions were grossly inadequate constituted degrading treatment in violation of Art.3 (*Price v UK* (2001)).

Racial harassment

Racial harassment has been found capable of being degrading
treatment (*Hilton v UK* (1976)). In *East African Asians v UK* (1973),
the Commission concluded that "the racial discrimination, to
which the applicants have been publicly subjected by the application of immigration legislation, constitutes an interference with
their human dignity". This amounted to degrading treatment in
violation of Art.3. For there to be a violation of Art.3, the state
must first intend to degrade someone (*Abdulaziz, Cabales and
Balkandali v UK* (1985)).

Discrimination

Discrimination against illegitimate children was found not to be
a violation of Art.3 in *Marcx v Belgium* (1979). Requiring wearing
of uniform by prisoners was not a breach of Art.3 (*Campbell v UK*
(1988)).

Corporal punishment of juveniles

The court found that the practice of birching young offenders on
the Isle of Man was a breach of Art.3 as constituting degrading
punishment: "A punishment does not lose its degrading character just because it is believed to be, or actually is, an effective

deterrent or aid to crime control" (*Tyrer v UK* (1978)). Corporal punishment in schools came under challenge in *Campbell and Cosans v UK* (1982), brought by the mothers of two Scots schoolboys threatened by the tawse. The court found it had not been established that pupils at schools where the tawse was in use were humiliated or debased in the eyes of others if they were punished with it. However, the failure to respect the parents' wishes that their sons not be beaten was a violation of Protocol 1, Art.2.

A series of subsequent cases narrowed the scope of permissible corporal punishment and eventually led the government to ban its use in state schools (*X v UK* (1981); *Warwick v UK* (1986); *Y v UK* (1992)). Its use in independent schools came under attack in *Costello-Roberts v UK* (1995), brought by a seven-year-old boy beaten with a gym shoe, who claimed a violation of Art.3. The punishment did not meet the minimum level of severity required to breach the Article. But the adverse effects on the complainant's physical and moral integrity amounted to a breach of Art.8.

A v UK (1999) was an action by a boy whose stepfather regularly beat him with a garden cane causing considerable bruising. The father was acquitted of assault on the basis that the beatings amount to reasonable chastisement, and the boy complained that the State had failed to safeguard his rights under Art.3. The court found that the boy's treatment did reach the level of severity prohibited by the Article and that the law allowing "reasonable chastisement" did not provide adequate protection to children's Convention rights.

SLAVERY AND FORCED LABOUR

Article 4 deals with two forms of activity; firstly, slavery or servitude and secondly, forced or compulsory labour. No derogation is allowed. Few cases have been heard on this Article.

Slavery and servitude

These conditions may occur when an individual is faced with a far-reaching oppressive control from which he cannot get free. In servitude as opposed to slavery there is no claim of ownership of the person. In *W, X, Y and Z v UK* (1967), the applicants were all young men who had joined the army or navy at the age of 15 or 16 for nine years, calculated from when they reached 18. They claimed violations of Arts 4, 6, 8 and 13. They petitioned for discharge under Art.4 from "oppressive compulsory service tantamount to the status of servitude". The government claimed the exception in the Article for "service of a military character" but the Commission stated that this, and the other three exceptions in para.3, applied only to "forced or compulsory labour". Since the parents had given consent to the enlisting, the work or service had no compulsory character. There was then no violation of Art.4. In an interesting example of its jurisprudential approach, the Commission drew on the background to the provision including Convention No.29 of the International Labour Organisation concerning Forced or Compulsory Labour, 1930.

Forced or compulsory labour

The court has only found one violation of the prohibition on forced or compulsory labour. This was mainly on the grounds of sex discrimination. In *Karlheinz Schmidt v Germany* (1994), there was a violation since the government required only male citizens to serve in the fire brigade or pay a fee in lieu.

The definition of forced or compulsory labour was taken from the conventions of the International Labour Organisation. Specifically, it must be performed involuntarily and the requirement to do the work must be unjust or oppressive or the work itself must involve avoidable hardship. This was applied in *Van der Mussele v Belgium* (1983). A young barrister complained that the obligation to represent pauper defendants, without being compensated for the work or reimbursed for expenditures involved, constituted a violation of Art.4(2). The Court noted that the work was not outside the scope of the applicant's normal duties, that the provision of services contributed to professional development and that the amount required was not too burdensome. The requirement also helped fulfil Belgium's obligations under Art.6 guaranteeing the right to counsel.

In *Van Droogenbroeck v Belgium* (1982), the court found that a prison sentence of two years followed by 10 years "at the government's disposal" did not amount to a violation of Art.4. *Harper v UK* (1985) was dismissed as an ill-founded claim. It concerned a change in the compulsory retirement age. Similarly *X v UK* (1968), concerning compulsory labour in prison, failed.

5. DUE PROCESS AND A FAIR TRIAL

The rights of those facing criminal or civil proceedings, arrest, incarceration or other penalty are affected by the operation of Arts 5, 6 and 7 and related Protocols. They are largely concerned with procedural and evidential matters, that is issues of due process. Article 6 is one of the most litigated Articles.

LIBERTY AND SECURITY OF THE PERSON

Article 5 and Arts 1–3 of Protocol No.4 preserve an individual's physical liberty and security and especially freedom from arbitrary arrest and detention.

When is detention lawful?

Article 5(1) lists an exhaustive closed set of six exceptions to the general rule that liberty and security of the person must be safeguarded. The paragraph is interpreted narrowly. A state may act to detain someone only "in accordance with a procedure prescribed by law", whether civil or criminal. Even if an individual waives his rights under the Article and agrees to his detention that detention can still be unlawful. In *De Wilde v Belgium* (1971), the court stated that the "right to liberty is too important in a 'democratic society' within the meaning of the Convention for a person to lose the benefit of the protection of the Convention for the single reason that he gives himself up to be taken into detention".

Articles 5(1)(a) and (c) fall within the scope of the criminal law. What is meant by "detention of a person after conviction by a competent court" Art.5(1)(a) was considered by the Strasbourg court in *Monnell and Morris v UK* (1988). The order by the Court of Appeal that some of the time spent in custody after conviction by the applicants should not count towards their sentences did impose in effect an additional period of imprisonment. However, the order fell within the definition under Art.5 and thus the article was not violated in this case.

In *Fox, Campbell and Harley v UK* (1988) the Strasbourg court considered the meaning of "reasonable suspicion" in Art.5(1)(c). The paragraph permits the lawful arrest of a person effected for the purpose of bringing him before the competent legal authority on reasonable suspicion of having committed an offence or when it is reasonably considered necessary to prevent his committing an offence or fleeing after having done so. It acknowledged that reasonable suspicion was not "a genuine and bona fide suspicion" and that in terrorist crimes, such as here, the police may have to act on the basis of information which cannot be revealed to the suspect. But the failure of the UK government to furnish material to indicate what was the basis of the suspicion, other than the previous convictions of the applicants, was a violation of Art.5(1)(c).

Articles 5(1)(b), (d), (e) and (f) all cover detention under the civil law, permitting it for such reasons as ensuring a witness attends a trial, a person of "unsound mind" is kept in a psychiatric hospital, failure to obey a court order, or in the case of minors, for "educational supervision". The Commission found that magistrates had acted within their jurisdiction in ordering an unemployed man to be detained following his failure to pay the community charge tax (*Benham v UK* (1996)). Article 5(1)(f) permits detention in immigration, asylum and extradition cases. The right of political asylum is not a right acknowledged by the ECHR but the state must not act in an arbitrary manner. Article 1, Protocol 4 (not ratified by the UK) specifically prohibits "deprivation of liberty merely on the ground of inability to fulfil a contractual obligation".

What are the procedural guarantees?

Article 5(2) ensures the right of the arrested person to be informed promptly of the reasons for the arrest and charged in a language he or she understands. This is to enable a person arrested to challenge the lawfulness of the detention (*X v UK* (1982)). Anyone arrested should be brought promptly before a judge or other judicial officer and should be tried within a reasonable time or released pending trial. In *Brogan and Others v UK* (1989), the court considered that detention for periods of over four days without charge and without being brought before a judge was a breach of Art.5(3). As a result of this case the UK issued a notice of derogation. (See also p.18).

The detained person has a right to have the lawfulness of his detention reviewed by a body independent of the executive and the parties (Art.5(4)). Successful challenges under this provision have been made in relation to continuing detention in discretionary period life sentences (*Weeks v UK* (1984); *Thynne v UK* (1990)) and to young people convicted of murder (*T & V v UK* (1999)). It was crucial to recognise circumstances could change over time (see also *Curley v UK* (2000)). As Feldman puts it,

> ". . . the European Court of Human Rights has impelled parliament
> and successive governments to impose a degree of order and
> regularity on the operation of discretionary life sentences and the
> detention of juvenile murderers." (*Civil Liberties and Human Rights in
> England and Wales* (2nd Ed. (2002) p.451).

The determinate sentences of criminal offenders itself, however, falls outside the scope of the Convention. *Wynne v UK* (1994). However, the procedure for sentencing has been challenged successfully in *R. v Offen* (2001). The Court of Appeal considered the statutory power to impose an automatic life sentence on a person convicted of a serious offence unless there were "exceptional circumstances". It interpreted the statute to mean that such a sentence should not be imposed where the offender "did not constitute a significant risk to the public". This liberal interpretation has been applied in a number of cases. Article 5(1)(f) was considered by the House of Lords in *(Saadi and Others) v Secretary of State for the Home Department* (2002). It held that the temporary detention of asylum seekers for the purpose of processing asylum applications was proportionate and reasonable.

Mentally ill patients

In *Stanley Johnson v UK* (1995), the court held that the retention at Rampton of a man who was no longer suffering from a mental disorder because no hostel accommodation could be found for him was a violation of Art.5(1)(e). In *R. (H) v Mental Health Review Tribunal* (2001) the Court of Appeal held that sections of the Mental Health Act 1983 were incompatible with Art.5(1) and (4) of the Convention. The sections placed the burden of proof on the patient to show that the conditions for continued detention were no longer satisfied. (See also *R. (von Brandenburg) v East London and City Mental Health NHS Trust* (2001).

Bail

An illustration of the impact of the Convention is *Cabellero v UK* (2000). As a result of this case the bail provisions under s.25 Criminal Justice and Public Order Act 1994 were amended. The original provisions were a breach of Art.5(3). In *Burgess v Home Office* (2001) Lord Phillips M.R. in the Court of Appeal found that Art.5 "added nothing to the claimant's case" for having a period of custody during trial deducted from his sentence.

Deportations

In *Zamir v UK* (1983), the court found that the procedure for challenging detention while awaiting deportation was a violation of Art.5. This was because of the seven weeks delay before a hearing after the application of a writ of habeas corpus and the lack of legal aid (see also *Chahal v UK* (1997)).

RIGHT TO A FAIR TRIAL

General features

Article 6 concerns the right to a fair trial. The common law equivalent is the doctrine of "natural justice", which like Art.6 applies in both a civil and a criminal law context. The Article is a natural progression from Art.5, which sets out the procedure under which a person may lawfully be deprived of personal liberty in many cases in anticipation or as a result of a civil or criminal hearing. The provisions of the two Articles, therefore, to some extent overlap. The wording of Article 6 is complex and some of the terminology needs to be analysed carefully before transposing into English law. Article 6(1) applies to both civil and criminal proceedings whereas Articles 6(2) and 6(3) apply only to criminal proceedings. These latter two are supplementary and give some specific but not exhaustive instances of specific requirements of a fair criminal trial. Thus, they amplify what is meant in Art.6(1) by a "fair and public hearing within a reasonable time by an independent and impartial tribunal established by law". The case law demonstrates that the Strasbourg court and the Commission have drawn on Art.6(2) and (3) in examining the fairness of civil proceedings also and have gone beyond Art.6(3) and 6(3) in identifying the content of a fair hearing. Article 6(1) in other words has not been applied restrictively (*Moreira de Azevedo v Portugal* (1990)).

The courts have examined the application of Art.6 in considering the division between administrative and judicial functions. In *Runa Begum v Tower Hamlets* (2003) a homeless person objected to the council accommodation she was offered. Her objection was rejected on statutory review by a council official and she appealed to the county court on the basis that the lack of independence of the reviewing officer infringed her Art.6 rights. The House of Lords decided that the officer was manifestly not an independent tribunal, since she was a council official reviewing the council's own decision. But it was not a breach of Art.6(1) for the decision to be taken by a tribunal which did not itself possess the necessary independence provided measures were in place to safeguard the fairness of the proceedings and the decision was subject to ultimate judicial control by a an independent court.

Supreme Court

The government has decided to create a Supreme Court for the United Kingdom, to replace the judicial committee of the House of Lords as a final court of appeal for all parts of the UK. In parallel moves, it has begun the process of abolishing the office of Lord Chancellor, begun a consultation process on a new way of appointing judges, and suspended appointment of new Queen's Counsel. These moves are to some extent founded on the need to meet the standards set by Art.6(1) of the Convention, which is perceived as requiring separation of powers. Separation of powers is a principle of the United States constitution which has not to the same extent been part of the United Kingdom system. There is a substantial irony in the fact that the Convention, originally drafted by Conservative English lawyers with the intention of bringing the benefits of the rule of law to post-war continental Europe, has become the instrument of sweeping constitutional change in the United Kingdom itself. Certainly this outcome was never foreseen by the Convention's authors. However, in *Stafford v UK* (2002) the Strasbourg court observed that "the notion of separation of powers between the executive and the judiciary ... has assumed growing importance in [our] case-law". And in *Benjamin and Wilson v UK* (2003), separation of powers is described as a "fundamental principle".

The traditional absence of separation of powers was epitomised by the office of Lord Chancellor which embodied judicial, executive and legislative power in a single individual, at the same time a judge, a Cabinet minister and a peer of the realm. The Lords of Appeal in Ordinary, too, who sit as the judicial committee of the House of Lords, are both judges and peers, sharing judicial and legislative roles. But the government has made clear its desire to "reflect and enhance the independence of the judiciary from both the legislature and the executive", in the consultation document *A Supreme Court for the United Kingdom* (CP 11/03). A number of decided cases have pushed the government down this road. Perhaps the most influential was *R. v Bow Street Metropolitan Magistrate, Ex p. Pinochet* (1999). In that case lawyers for the former Chilean dictator successfully challenged the fact that Lord Hoffmann was sitting on his extradition hearing while chairman of the Amnesty International Charity Trust. Possible conflicts of interest between the Law Lords' judicial and legislative roles were also highlighted in *R. v Secretary of State for the Home Department, Ex p. Fire Brigades Union* (1995), in which a bench was only constituted with difficulty because so many Law Lords had spoken in the House of Lords against the proposals for criminal injury compensation which were under review. Lord Hoffmann had to stand down a second time, in a libel action brought by a former Irish prime minister, because of his involvement in pushing the Defamation Act 1996 through parliament. Even in *Pepper v Hart* (1993), which concerned the extent to which Hansard could be used as aid to interpretation of statutes, there was concern because several of the Law Lords had spoken about the issue in strong terms during a debate two years before. Since 2000 the Law Lords have bound themselves not to involve themselves in strong party political disputes or speak about matters they might have to decide as a judge. But drawing the line has proved difficult.

Appointment of Appeal Court judges and Law Lords is by the Queen on the advice of the Prime Minister. Other judges are appointed either by the Queen on the advice of the Lord Chancellor or by the Lord Chancellor on his own authority. The system is administered by the Department for Constitutional Affairs. Since 2001 the system has been overseen by a Commission on Judicial Appointments. The government has proposed to strengthen the role of the Commission so as to bolster judicial independence and enhance public confidence in the judiciary. It has opened public consultation on whether the commission should itself appoint the judges, whether it should make recommendations to the Queen, or some mixture of the two. There is also an issue of the parliamentary accountability of the Secretary of State for Constitutional Affairs in the judicial appointment process.

The abolition of Queen's Counsel was the subject of a consultation paper in July 2003, and the government appointed no Q.C.s in 2004. The anomaly that the top rank of a supposedly independent profession should be appointed by a government minister is highlighted in the consultation paper, which questions whether silk is an adequate guarantee of quality and whether the current system serves the interests of consumers of legal services.

Access to the courts

A fundamental requirement of Art.6 is that there should be access to a judicial procedure. The difference between procedural rights, protected by Art.6, and substantive law rights, has been a matter of controversy. In *Osman v United Kingdom* (2000) the Strasbourg Court had held that the immunity of the police from suits in negligence violated Art.6 but it subsequently retracted from this approach. In the House of Lords decision *Barrett v Enfield* (1999) Lord Browne-Wilkinson criticised *Osman* arguing that the ECtHR had misunderstood the relevant case law. In *Z v United Kingdom* (2001) the European Court of Human Rights accepted that such immunities were matters of substantive law on which it was not appropriate for the ECtHR to pronounce. In *Matthews v Ministry of Defence* (2003) the House of Lords held that the immunity of the Crown in tort is a matter of substantive not procedural law and does not amount to a violation of Art.6. The judicial review approach has been criticised by the EctHR. It held in *Kingsley v UK* (2001) that the failure to consider the merits of the decision violated Art.6. (see also *R. (Beeson) v Dorset CC* (2003)).

What is the meaning of "civil rights and obligations"?

This is not considered only by reference to the procedure set out under domestic law of the state but by an analysis of the right itself. Where a right is set out in the domestic law of a state the court will acknowledge it as a civil right but the definition is not always the same as that of the law of the country concerned (*James v UK* (1986)). Examples of where the court has identified civil rights are: libel hearings affecting the right to enjoy honour and good reputation (*Tolstoy Miloslavsky v UK* (1995)); disciplinary hearings of the General Medical Council affecting the right to practice a profession (*Wickramsinghe v UK* (1998)); proceedings before an appeals board to continue getting health insurance allowance (*Feldbrugge v The Netherlands* (1986)).

Property rights concern civil rights and these will include planning determinations and following *Gaygasuz v Austria* (1996), an emergency assistance benefit which had a contributory element. See the House of Lords decision in *R. (Alconbury Developments Ltd) v Secretary of State for the Environment, Transport and Regions* (2001).

Civil or public law right?

A restrictive feature of the Strasbourg jurisprudence is that public law rights are not embraced within the definition of civil rights and do not enjoy the protection of Art.6. Examples of public law rights are administrative proceedings on categorisation of prisoners (*Brady v UK* (1980)), deportation decisions (*Uppal and Others v UK (No 2)* (1988)) and hearings concerning public employment (*Balfour v UK* (1997)). In the latter case a former diplomat failed to gain the protection of Art.6 in his challenge to his employers' use of the doctrine of public interest immunity in his unfair dismissal hearing. In *Pellegrin v France* (2001) the Grand Chamber developed a more liberal test based on functions not status. In *Devlin v UK* (2001) it held there was a breach of Art.6 in the failure of the Secretary of State to adduce evidence of the applicant's unsuitability for the civil service before the employment tribunal. Disputes over pecuniary matters such as pensions involving public officials may come under Art.6 (*Lombardo v Italy* (1996)) although disputes over recruitment, careers and termination do not. The definition of public employees excludes those who are not technically civil servants. Thus, in *C v UK* (1987), a school caretaker was entitled to claim Art.6 protection. The Commission noted:

> " ... whilst internal professional disciplinary proceedings against persons employed in public service may not attract the guarantees of Article 6 paragraph 1 of the Convention, when a contract of employment, albeit in the public service, permits access to the civil courts to determine the respective civil liabilities of the parties, the proceedings before the normal courts may usually be said to determine civil rights and obligations within the meaning of Article 6 paragraph 1 of the Convention ... ".

Article 6 and employment law

Article 6 is not engaged with regard to internal disciplinary hearings (*Darnell v UK* (1994)), but may be engaged in professional disciplinary tribunals, see *R. v UK Central Council for Nursing, Midwifery and Health Visiting, Ex p. Tehrani* (2001).

What is a "criminal charge"?

The full range of Art.6 rights is available only for criminal charges. In *Eckle v Federal Republic of Germany* (1982), the court defined a criminal charge as "an official notification given to an individual by the competent authority of an allegation that he has committed a criminal offence". This has been extended to include measures which "substantially affect the situation of the suspect" (*Foti and Others v Italy* (1982)). In *McFeeley v UK* (1981), the Commission considered whether Art.6 applied to the disciplinary adjudications of the prison governor; relevant factors included the degree of severity of the penalty and whether the provisions defining the offence charged belonged, according to the legal system of the respondent state, to criminal law, disciplinary law or both concurrently. In *McIntosh v HM. Advocate* (2001) the Privy Council held that confiscation proceedings arising from drug offences do not constitute a criminal charge. (See also *Phillips v UK* (2001)). In *McCann v Manchester Crown Court* (2002) the House of Lords held that Anti-Social Behaviour Orders were civil in nature, although the applicant for the order should prove the case to the criminal standard.

The meaning of "determination of a right or charge"

This has been taken to mean that some form of judicial scrutiny must be available.

Equality of arms

This is the idea that each side in the proceedings should have the same opportunity to put their case and neither should have a considerable advantage. This includes access to relevant documents, information about relevant dates, and in most circumstances attendance of defendants (*Monnell and Morris v UK* (1987)).

Independent and impartial tribunal established by law

This principle enshrines the separation of powers but it is left to the individual states to determine how it should be applied. It is vital that judges should not be bound by the interpretations of the law made by the executive. In *Beaumartin v France* (1994), there was a violation of Art.6(1) where a court asked the Minister of Foreign Affairs to interpret a treaty and used that interpretation to dismiss the claim.

There is no specific requirement of trial by jury. Where there are jurors they must be independent and impartial. There was no violation however where a jury had allegedly made negative remarks about a member of the racial minority to which the defendant belonged which the judge had countered with clear directions to the jury (*Gregory v UK* (1997)). In *R. v Secretary of State for the Home Department Ex p. Anderson* (2002) the House of Lords held that the involvement of the Home Secretary in fixing the length of imprisonment for those convicted of murder was incompatible with Art.6(1). This followed *Stafford v UK* (2002).

Within a reasonable time

This applies in civil and criminal cases, and relevant common factors include the complexity of the case, any behaviour of the applicant which may have contributed to delay and any special circumstances. In relation to criminal trials, time begins to run when there has been official notification "to an individual by a competent authority of an allegation that he has committed a criminal offence" (*De Weer v Belgium* (1980)). It is not necessary for formal charges to have been laid: the test is whether "the situation of the person concerned has been substantially affected as a result of a suspicion against him" (*X v Austria* (1967); *Eckle v Germany* (1982)). In civil proceedings the court has generally allowed the states more licence. There was a violation in *Darnell v UK* (1993), where after dismissal by an area health authority in 1984, the applicant faced nine years of legal proceedings including judicial review applications and hearings in an industrial tribunal and the Employment Appeal tribunal.

A public hearing

This requirement may be excluded in:

> "... the interests of morals, public order or national security in a democratic society, where the interests of juveniles or the protection of the private life of the parties so require or to the extent strictly necessary in the opinion of the court in special circumstances where publicity would prejudice the interests of justice".

However, there is an unqualified right to public pronouncement of the judgment. The reason behind the requirement of public hearings is not only to serve the interests of the parties but also to inspire confidence in the legal system among the public as a whole.

The presumption of innocence

A fundamental aspect of a fair trial is the requirement of the state to prove its case against the defendant. The state should run the risk of losing. Before conviction the defendant is innocent, so there was a violation of Art.6(2) when a government official and a policeman publicly declared a suspect to be guilty before charges were preferred (*Allenet de Ribemont v France* (1995)). The provision does not however mean that the burden of proof must always be on the prosecutor. Presumptions of law or fact in favour of the prosecution, such as the principle of strict liability, are acceptable "within reasonable limits" (*Salabiaku v France* (1988)). It is therefore unlikely that the requirement under Art.6 will be different from the existing common law position, which accepted that the burden could shift by implication.

Parliament of course may expressly shift the burden. In *R. v DPP, Ex p. Kebilene* (1999), the House of Lords was asked to consider whether the reverse burden provisions in the Prevention of Terrorism Act violated Art.6(2). In the Divisional Court Lord Bingham had decided that these sections "in a blatant and obvious way undermined the presumption of innocence". The House of Lords did not see the need to pronounce on this point since it decided that judicial review was not available in this case. However, several of the speeches noted the effect of Art.6(2). Lord Hope pointed out that in considering whether a statutory provision had shifted the legal burden of proof, account should be taken of the problem the legislation was designed to address. He stated: "As a matter of general principle therefore a fair balance must be struck between the demands of the general interest of the community and the protections of the fundamental rights of the individual". One factor was whether the defendant was being required to prove an essential element of the offence or establish a special defence of exception, which would be less objectionable.

The House of Lords again considered the presumption of innocence in *R. v Lambert (Steven)* (2002). Section 28(2) of the Misuse of Drugs Act 1971 provides that where a defendant is found with drugs in his possession it is a defence for the defendant to prove that he neither believed nor suspected that the substance in question was controlled. The House, reversing the Court of Appeal, held that in order to comply with Art.6(2) the section should be interpreted in this case as only imposing the evidential not the legal burden of proof on the defendant. It was not a justification or a proportionate response to the problem of illegal drugs to transfer the legal burden on the accused and require him to prove on the balance of probabilities that he did not know the bag contained a controlled drug. However, this interpretation did not help the applicant since his conviction predated the Act coming into force. The fact that this was a majority decision and the differing decisions of the Court of Appeal and the House of Lords illustrate contradictory views on the extent to which the state should be allowed to undermine the rights of defendant in the interests of protecting society against the social problem of drug dealing. (See also *R. v Benjafield* (2002))

Privilege against self-incrimination—general

The right not to incriminate oneself is not specifically included in the Convention. There are a number of aspects of this right which are however still protected in English law—these include the right of witnesses in a trial to refuse to answer questions which might lead to criminal charges. One aspect has, however, been excluded by statute over the years. The most controversial reforms were enacted by the Criminal Justice and Public Order Act 1994. In relation to pre-trial investigations a court or jury may now, under certain conditions, draw adverse inferences from the accused's failure to give information when being questioned by constables and those charged with the duty of investigating offences. The same consequences may follow from failure to testify. The case law has impacted on these developments in a number of ways.

ECHR and the right to silence

In a landmark case the court ruled that the convention included the right of anyone charged with a criminal offence to remain silent. Thus, the convictions of an applicant for failing to hand over bank statements to the French customs violated Art.6 (*Funke v France* (1993)). Again in *Saunders v UK* (1997), the court ruled that use at trial of incriminating statements obtained from the defendant by DTI inspectors using their compulsory powers was oppressive. His right to silence was undermined by the pressure to co-operate. However, the court has since shown that it does not regard the right to silence as an absolute principle. In *Murray v UK* (1996), it held that "the right to remain silent under police questioning and the privilege against self-incrimination are generally recognised international standards which lie at the heart of the notion of a fair procedure under Article 6". However, the drawing of adverse inferences from silence need not necessarily be an infringement. It depends on the circumstances of each case. It will require "particular regard to the situations where inferences may be drawn, the weight attached to them by the national courts in their assessment of the evidence and the degree of compulsion in the situation".

Murray arose from the provisions of the Criminal Evidence (Northern Ireland) Order 1988 which paralleled those in the Criminal Justice and Public Order Act. In the circumstances of the case there was very strong prosecution evidence which called for answers from the applicant and it was not unfair to draw "common sense" inferences from his failure to provide an explanation. In a subsequent decision the court held that it was of paramount importance that the judge should give specific directions on what adverse inferences, if any, might be drawn. The absence of such a direction will constitute a violation of Art.6(1) (*Condron v UK* (1999)).

In *Condron* the accused's solicitor advised them to remain silent because he deemed them to be unfit for interview due to their drug withdrawal symptoms. The drawing of adverse inferences in such circumstances was not in itself a violation, but a crucial question is the directions to the jury. It is clear from *Saunders v UK* that privilege against self-incrimination which is implicit in Art.6 does not extent to refusal to co-operate in a procedure which may yield incriminating evidence such as a breathalyser test or the taking of a bodily sample. The argument was that, unlike verbal explanations, these had an existence independent of the will of the accused. This reasoning is however difficult to square with *Funke* since the documents there had an independent existence. In *Brown v Stott* (2001) the Privy Council held that the use in evidence of a dependant's compulsory admission of driving at the time a traffic offence was committed was not a violation of Art.6.

There was a clear public interest in enforcing drink driving legislation and in this instance some balancing of the general interests of the community against the rights of the individual was necessary. It seems that although the overall unqualified right to a fair trial cannot be balanced, any or all of its constituent elements can be balanced as long as the response is proportionate.

The Strasbourg Court again considered the question of inferences from the defendant's silence, particularly where the solicitor has advised silence. In *Beckles v UK* (2003) the defendant had remained silent on legal advice. The court held that there had been a breach of Art.6 since the judge had failed to direct the jury properly in particular by failure to emphasise that the jury should only draw adverse inferences where they considered the silence was consistent only with guilt. The Court of Appeal adopted a somewhat restrictive approach to the Strasbourg decision in *Beckles* in *R. v Howell* (2003). Here the defendant had remained silent on legal advice. The Court of Appeal suggested that silence was only admissible if circumstances such as "the suspect's condition (ill-health, in particular mental instability; confusion' intoxication; shock and so forth . . .) or his inability genuinely to recollect events without reference to documents which are not to hand, or communication with other persons who may be able to assist his recollection.

The ECtHR has also recognised that the suspect's right to silence may be compromised in other ways than the drawing of permissible inferences under the Criminal Justice and Public Order Act 1994. In *Allen v UK* (2003) the police planted an undercover informer in a cell with a suspect. He had remained silent under police questioning but made some incriminating statements to his cellmate. These were tape-recorded and admitted at trial. The ECtHR held that the suspect's right to silence "is effectively undermined" in such circumstances but they went on to say that these circumstances were confined to cases "where the informant was acting as an agent of the state at the time when the accused made the statement and were it was the informer who caused the accused to make the statement" and this was such a case. Since the normal procedural safeguards of giving a caution or allowing access to legal advice were not present there was a violation of Art.6.

The right to be informed promptly, in a language which the accused understands, and in detail, of the charge

Provision of a defence counsel capable of communicating in both the language of the court and the language of the applicant will fulfil this requirement (*Kanasinghe v Austria* (1989)).

The right to adequate time and facilities for the preparation of the defence

The accused may argue that this provision requires an opportunity to confer with a legal adviser. In *Campbell and Fells v UK* (1984), the applicants claimed a violation of this provision since the police or other authorities sit in on consultations between defendants and their solicitors. The court accepted that in principle those consultations should be conducted in private but that there were exceptional circumstances where this need not be so, if, for example, there were reasonable grounds to suspect counsel was abusing his professional position, for example, by colluding with his client to destroy evidence. In *S v Switzerland* (1991), the court held that "free communication between a lawyer and his detained client is a fundamental right which is essential in a democratic society above all in the most serious of cases".

The right to defend oneself through legal assistance or through legal aid

In *Murray v UK* (1996), the delay of 48 hours in access to a solicitor was a violation of Art.6(3). As a result UK law was amended so that inferences from silence when questioned are now only admissible if the accused had been offered an opportunity to consult a solicitor (Criminal Justice and Public Order Act, ss.34–37). The requirement for legal assistance will vary according to the complexity of the case. In *Granger v UK* (1990), the applicant had his request for costs for legal representation turned down at an oral appellate hearing against a conviction for perjury. This was a violation of Arts 6(1) and 6(3)(c). The UK practice has also been found inadequate in *Bower v UK* (1994) and *Maxwell v UK* (1994). In *Benham v UK* (1996), the lack of availability of full legal aid for a committal hearing in a poll tax case was a violation of Art.6(3)(c) as well as 6(1). Regard was had to the complexity of the issues and the severity of the penalty. Legal aid is not available for some criminal charges under English law and it may be that this will not satisfy a claim under Art.6.

Legal Professional Privilege

In *Brenner v UK* (2002) the ECtHR reviewed the facilities or solicitor-client interviews in police stations and the judgment had implications for the protection of legal professional privilege under the Human Rights Act. In this case the police had refused to allow the applicant to have access to his lawyer for the first 24 hours of detention and questioning and after that had only permitted him to confer with the lawyer in the presence of a police officer. This was held to be a breach of Art.6(1) and (3)(c). It was not sufficient that it was a case of suspected terrorism and that there was a fear that lawyers might pass information to other suspects. The right of access to a lawyer may be restricted for good cause but the reasons must be based on the facts of the particular case.

The right to confront witnesses

This right is intimately related to the equality of arms principle, which is fundamental to Art.6. In some cases the court has found a violation where the testimony of anonymous witnesses was permitted, such witnesses being unavailable for questioning by the defence (see, for example, *Saidi v France* (1993)). However this is a difficult area, especially in view of the need to protect vulnerable witnesses, particularly victims. Thus, in *Doorson v Netherlands* (1996), prosecution witnesses who claimed they were intimidated by the defendants were allowed to give evidence at a pre-trial hearing. The defendant was not present but his counsel could cross-examine. The interests of victims, in other words, must also be safeguarded—they have rights under Art.5 (to liberty and security) and Art.8 (privacy). The Court held: "Against this background principles of fair trial also require that in appropriate cases the interests of the defendant are balances against those of witnesses, or victims, called upon to testify". The potential clash between these interests has arisen on a number of issues relating to rape trials. Under s.41 of the Youth Justice and Criminal Evidence Act defendants are not allowed to cross-examine an alleged victim in person and cross-examination on the sexual history of the complainant, including sexual relations between defendant and victim, is curtailed.

In *R. v A (No.2)* (2001) the House of Lords addressed the following question, "May a sexual relationship between a defendant and complainant be relevant to the issue of consent so as to render its exclusion under s.41 of the Youth Justice and Criminal Evidence Act 1999 a contravention of the defendant's right to a fair trial?" The House considered that the defendant's prior relations with the complainant, although they might be relevant, could not be admitted under normal canons of statutory interpretation under s.41. It avoided making a declaration of incompatibility by creatively interpreting the section in a manner compatible with the demands of Art.6 of the Convention. (See also page 44.)

Admissibility of evidence: covert surveillance

Much discussion has centred on whether the Human Rights Act will require that illegally or improperly obtained evidence should be excluded by the provisions of Art.6. The case law suggests that the provisions of the Article require similar considerations to be raised as under the operation of s.78 of the Police and Criminal Evidence Act 1984 (PACE), discretion to exclude. The applicant in *Khan v UK* (2000) complained that by unlawfully bugging his house and obtaining incriminating conversations his rights under Art.6 and 8 were violated. The court found no violation of Art.6, adding that "had the domestic courts been of the view that the admission of the evidence would have given rise to substantive unfairness they would have had a discretion to exclude it under s.78 PACE". There was a breach of Art.8. See also *R. v P.* (2001) and *A.G.'s Reference (No.3 of 1999)* (2001) where no violations of Arts 6 or 8 were found by the House of Lords.

Admissibility of evidence: entrapment

English law does not allow a defence of entrapment but in principle such evidence may be excluded under s.78 of PACE. The key element is causation—has the accused been persuaded to do something he would not otherwise have done? Essentially the same approach is adopted by the European Court of Human Rights. In *Teixera de Castro v Portugal* (1998), the court held that a person was deprived of the right to a fair trial from the outset, in a case where he was incited by police officers to supply drugs to them in circumstances where he had no previous known connection with drug dealing. The position was different in a situation where police officers posed as potential purchasers in a drug deal which was already under way. In *R. v Shannon* (2001), the Court of Appeal considered that "The end result of *Teixera*, couched as it was in terms of incitement and causation, was not necessarily at odds with English law or inconsistent with *R. v Smurthwaite* (1994)". The trial judge had correctly exercised his discretion not to exclude the evidence of the supply of cannabis by the defendant to a journalist posing as an Arab sheikh.

In *R. v Looseley; Attorney-General's Reference (No.3 of 2000)* (2001) the House of Lords demonstrated strong judicial recognition of the dangers of excessive police behaviour in cases of entrapment and the need for the court to protect citizens. It held that in assessing whether to exclude evidence or stay criminal proceedings in cases of entrapment the requirements of Art.6 are compatible with s.78 PACE and the common law. Following this judgment the focus of the courts' approach must be on an objective assessment of the conduct of the police rather than the predisposition of the defendant. Lord Hoffmann stressed the importance of the "protection of the integrity of the criminal justice system" and Lord Nicholls specifically recognised that *R. v Sang* (1980) had been "overtaken" by statute and case law. It was not a violation of Convention rights to provide a person with an "unexceptional" opportunity to commit an offence but if there has been an abuse of state power then the appropriate remedy is a stay of the indictment rather than exclusion of evidence under s.78.

Admissibility of evidence: disclosure

The failure to disclose evidence which might help the defence has led to a number of miscarriages of justice in the past (see for example *R. v Ward* (1993)). The legal framework now governing the procedure is a mixture of statute, Attorney-Generals' guidelines and common law. In addition the right of pre-trial disclosure is a component of the right to a fair trial under Art.6(1). The Criminal Courts Review by Lord Justice Auld made proposals for reform of the law. In *R. v Botmeh and Alami* (2001) the Court of Appeal rejected the argument that it was contrary to Art.6 for it to hold an *ex parte* public interest immunity hearing into evidence whose existence the prosecution had denied during the trial. The Court of Appeal's function was to assess the safety of the conviction and a finding of unfairness at trial did not necessarily mean the convictions should be quashed. The doctrine of public interest immunity (PII) enables sensitive material, which may harm the public interest, to be suppressed. In *Rowe and Davis v UK* (2000), the court found there had been a violation of Art.6(1). By contrast in *Jasper v UK, Fitt v UK* (2000) there was no violation of Art.6(1) since the defence were notified of the *ex parte* hearing and were allowed to present their case to the judge. In *Edwards v UK* (1992) the European Court of Human Rights stated that fairness required disclosure to the defendant of all the material evidence for or against the accused. As a result of the decision in *Rowe* and *Davis* changes have been made to the procedure for claiming public interest immunity.

Article 7 is concerned with retrospective legislation. In *S.W. v UK* (1995) there was no violation of Art.7 in a conviction for rape of a wife which marked "the abandonment of the unacceptable idea of a husband being immune against prosecution for rape of his wife". There was a violation however in *Welch v UK* (1995) in the confiscation of property under a statute passed after the conviction for the crime. See also *R. (Uttley) v Secretary of State for the Home Department* (2003), holding that a period of licence imposed under the Criminal Justice Act 1991 for offences committed before the implementation of the Act was incompatible with prisoners' rights under Art.7.

Duty to give reasons

The Strasbourg jurisprudence has underlined the need for courts to give reasons for their judgments and the domestic courts have acknowledged that since the coming into force of the Human Rights Act there is an enhanced duty to give reasons to comply with the ECHR. In response to this *Practice Direction (Justices: Clerks to Court)* (2000) sets out guidelines for magistrates. Crown Courts and magistrates now generally give reasons on questions of admissibility and submissions of no case to answer. The protection offered by Strasbourg in this area is limited. In *Hiro Balani v Spain* (1995) the court noted that Art.6(1) obliges courts to give reasons for their judgments, but cannot be understood as requiring a detailed answer to every argument. The extent to which this duty to give reasons applies may vary according to the nature of the decision. Breaches of the obligation to state reasons could only be determined in the light of the circumstances of the case.

---

6. PRIVACY, MARRIAGE, PROPERTY

General features

The purpose of Arts 8, 12 and Protocol 1, Art.1 is to protect privacy, family life, home and correspondence, the right to marry and found a family, the equality of spouses and property. They have raised complicated questions of what is meant by "private life", "family" and "home". The effect of incorporation is wide sweeping for two reasons. Firstly, English law has traditionally given little respect for privacy as a free standing right, and secondly, since these are essentially individual rights they potentially involve conflict with other competing interests, such as that of the public in accessing information about the activities of individuals. Examples of groups who are likely to be affected by Art.8 include those whose homes are threatened by pollution, homosexual couples who wish to be defined as a family for housing or adoption, and employees who are subject to intrusive surveillance. The rights under Art.8 are qualified.

PRIVACY

Positive as well as negative obligations

Article 8(2) specifies that "there shall be no interference by a public authority in the exercise of this right". This has been interpreted by the court to imply a positive duty to ensure respect for certain rights. In *Johnston and Others v Ireland* (1986), it was argued by a child's parents that the state's ban on divorce made it impossible for them to legitimise their child by marriage because one parent had been previously married. The court held that there was a breach of Art.8 in that the child was treated in a different way from a legitimate child. While the ban on divorce was not itself a breach of the Article, the state had a duty to give protection to children born out of wedlock. Again, in *Airey v Ireland* (1979), in ruling that there was a violation of Art.8 in the failure of the state to make legal aid available to a woman wishing to obtain a decree of judicial separation, the court declared:

> "Although the object of Article 8 is essentially that of protecting the individual against arbitrary interference by the public authorities, it does not merely compel the state to abstain from such interference. In addition to this primarily negative undertaking, there may be positive obligations inherent in an effective respect for private and family life".

English law and privacy

See pp.58–61.

Respect for private life

This has been interpreted to include not only personal autonomy but also relations with others. "Respect for private life must also comprise to a certain degree the right to establish and develop relationships with human beings" (*Niemetz v Germany* (1992)). Thus it has an impact on sexual relations and on practices at work.

Violence

The right to respect for private life may be violated by violence which falls short of the level required for Art.3. Thus, in *X and Y v Netherlands* (1985), the sexual assault of a young mentally handicapped woman while in a private care home and the refusal to sanction a prosecution was a violation of Art.8. It was a "case where fundamental values and aspects of private life are at stake. Effective deterrence is indispensable in this area and it can be achieved only by criminal law provisions". However, in *Costello-Roberts v UK* (1993), corporal punishment carried out on a private school pupil by a member of staff "did not entail adverse effects [to the child's] physical or moral integrity sufficient to bring it within the scope of the prohibition contained in Article 8".

Medical Law

The Human Rights Act is having an increasing impact on medical and the number of cases have conceded the relevance of the Art.8 as well as that of Arts 2 and 3. In *R. v DPP, Ex p. Pretty* (2002) (see also p.67) the House of Lords held that Art.8 was not engaged since claims under Arts 2 and 3 had failed. Alternatively, it was held that even if there had been a breach of Art.8 such interference was justified for protecting the rights of others, specifically vulnerable people. A number of domestic cases have required the domestic courts to adjudicate between claims made by private parties. Obviously such a rival claims would not be at issue in the Strasbourg Court since these involve individuals making claims against the state. A challenge to the Human Fertilisation and Embryology Act failed. In *Evans v Human Fertilisation and Embryology Authority* (2003) the court rejected the argument of the claimant contesting the right of her former partner to refuse consent to the use of embryos for implantation. Both had referred to Art.8 in support of their arguments. The court held that the interference with the claimant's Art.8 rights was proportionate and necessary for the protection of all parties.

Homosexual relationships

In a number of cases the Commission and the court have found that a state's prohibition of homosexual acts between consenting adults was a violation of Art.8. In *Dudgeon v UK* (1981), the court found that the criminalisation of all homosexual behaviour in Northern Ireland was disproportionate to any possible legitimate aims of the government and that a sexual life was "a most intimate aspect" of a person's private life. This, however, did not mean that prosecution of sado-masochistic practices was a violation (*Laskey, Jaggard and Brown v UK* (1997)). The UK had however violated the Convention in sanctioning Ministry of Defence enquiries into the sexual orientation of members of the services and their consequential discharge. In *Smith and Grady v UK* (2000), the court said that the Ministry of Defence could not refuse to take note of the views of other contracting states which allowed the admission of homosexuals into the armed forces. In addition, the Commission stated that the different ages of consent for heterosexuals and homosexuals was a violation of Art.8 in combination with Art.14.

Transsexuals

The position of transsexuals raises questions of privacy, family life and the right to marry. The court and the Commission have pronounced on all these areas and their approach has changed over the past 20 years. In *Rees v UK* (1986), the court, disagreeing with the Commission, held that there was no breach of Art.8 in the refusal of the UK government to alter a birth certificate of a woman who had undergone a sex change. As a result he was unable to marry. The court accepted that what was meant by "respect" for family life was not clear-cut. It noted that transsexuals were free to change their names and could be issued with official documents bearing their chosen first names and surnames and indicating their preferred sex by the relevant prefix (Mr, Mrs, Ms or Miss): "This freedom gives them a considerable advantage in comparison with States where all official documents have to conform with the records held by the registry office". However, unlike the position in some other countries there is no provision for legally valid civil status certificates, people have "on occasion to establish their identity by means of a birth certificate which is either an authenticated copy of or an extract from the birth register."

UK law recognised the applicant as a woman as far as marriage, pension rights and certain employments since the birth certificate was unamended. The court did not accept that the UK was required to change its system of registering births and determine civil status as other states did, since such a system "would have important administrative consequences and would impose new duties on the rest of the population". The court followed this reasoning in *Cossey v UK* (1990). However, in *B v France* (1992), the court took a different stance and acknowledged that the situation had changed since *Rees* and *Cossey*. The failure of the French authorities to annotate a birth certificate to note the change of sex of the applicant was a violation of the right to respect for private life. The court noted that this could be done without legislation (unlike the situation in the UK) and that French law and practice on civil status put a heavier burden on transsexuals than did the UK.

The change of approach was further developed in *Goodwin v UK* (2002). Two post-operative male to female transsexuals faced difficulties in matters such as pensions and national insurance because they were still regarded as legally male. In addition they suffered anxiety and humiliation. The Strasbourg court held there was a violation of Art.8 and 12. The government could no longer rely on a margin of appreciation in view of changes in attitudes to transsexuals. Following this decision, in *Bellinger v Bellinger* (2003) the House of Lords disturbed the existing legal position and declared s.11 (c) of the Matrimonial Causes Act 1973 incompatible with Arts 8 and 12. It held that the recognition of gender reassignment for the purpose of marriage was a matter for parliament which was to bring forward primary legislation to allow transsexual persons to marry in their acquired gender. This was done by means of the Gender Recognition Act 2004.

Privacy at work

An individual has a right to a "private life" at work. In *Niemetz v Germany* (1992), the District Court in Munich had issued a warrant to search a lawyer's office, in an effort to identify a third party responsible for writing an insulting letter to a judge. The warrant had been drawn in broad terms and there were no procedural safeguards. The applicant had his private life violated. In *Halford v UK* (1997), a former assistant chief constable of Merseyside police complained that the authorities were intercepting her private calls from work, made on an internal police telecommunications system. The UK government failed to convince the court that since the calls were made from Halford's workplace they were not covered by Art.8. The court held that "telephone calls made from business premises as well as from home may be covered by the notions of 'private life' and 'correspondence' within the meaning of Article 8(1)". The applicant had a reasonable expectation of privacy since she was not warned that her calls might be intercepted.

Surveillance

The state's surveillance of private individuals might violate several provisions of Art.8(1)—the right to respect for privacy, correspondence and for the home. In *Malone v UK* (1984), the court found against the British government for intercepting the phone calls of the applicant who was a dealer convicted of receiving stolen goods. There was then no statutory procedure for monitoring phone calls of private citizens. Therefore the interceptions were not in accordance with the law. The case led to the passing of the Interception of Communications Act 1985, but this did not cover internal telecommunications systems, hence the decision in *Halford*. The latter in turn has led to the Regulation of Investigatory Powers Act 2000, which affects the privacy of employees. The government may argue therefore that interference is now in accordance with the law, although it is still open to the courts to declare the statute incompatible with the Convention. In *Khan v UK* (2000), the placing of a listening device on premises attended by a suspected criminal was a violation of Art.8(1). Evidence obtained from CCTV is frequently used in criminal trials. See *R. v Loveridge and others* (2001) (see also pp.159–163).

Data collection/security vetting

States have generally been permitted quite a generous margin of appreciation in relation to the gathering of information other than in a criminal investigation. For example, in *Leander v Sweden* (1987), although the Swedish government's supply of secret information on the applicant to his prospective employers as a means of security vetting was an interference with the right to privacy, this was "necessary in a democratic society" since it was required for protecting national security. The actions against the applicant did not "constitute an obstacle to his leading a private life of [his] own choosing." There is thus no right of access to public service. In *Leander* the refusal to allow the applicant access to the information held on him was justified. However, in other circumstances this might not be so. Certain types of personal information might be essential to the right of a person to a private life. Thus in *Gaskin v UK* (1989), the applicant was denied access to files compiled while he was a child in the care of a local authority. The latter claimed to be protecting the confidentiality of third parties. This refusal, without any kind of independent check on the claim of third party confidentiality, was an infringement of the right to a private life.

Some disclosure of information to third parties may amount to a violation. In *X v Commission of the European Communities* (1995), an applicant for employment with the Commission had refused an AIDS test and was required to take a general blood test. This revealed that he was HIV positive and he was refused the job. The court upheld his claim. It held that the right to a private life is a fundamental right protected by the legal order of the Community and "includes in particular a person's right to keep his state of health secret". However, disclosure might be legitimate, as for example in *TV v Finland* (1993), where disclosure to prison staff of a prisoner's HIV status was justified in the interests of his health. In *MS v Sweden* (1997), medical records of an applicant were disclosed by a hospital to a social insurance office in a dispute over her claim for compensation for a work-related back injury. The interference with her right to privacy was justified as it served to protect the economic well being of the country. It has been suggested that the reasoning in this case may provide a basis for future challenges under Art.8 to covert video surveillance of personal injury claimants. Another justification for disclosure of private information to third parties is the process of civil litigation or criminal proceedings (see *Vermont v UK* (1999)).

The meaning of family life

"Family life" encompasses "at least the ties between near relatives, for instance those between grandparents and grandchildren, since such relatives may play a considerable part in family life", as the court put it in *Marckx v Belgium* (1979). It declared that legislation which discriminated against children born outside marriage was a violation of the right to respect for family life. In general, however, the view of family life is a conventional one. Homosexual and transsexual unions are not regarded as constituting family life. Thus, in *X v UK* (1997), the refusal to allow a transsexual to be registered as the father of a child conceived by his partner as a result of artificial insemination was not a breach of Art.8. In some respects English law predating the implementation of the Human Rights Act has been more progressive in defining the family. Thus, in *Fitzpatrick v Sterling Housing Ltd* (1999), the House of Lords held that a same-sex partner of a tenant was now to be recognised as capable of being a member of a tenant's family for the purpose of taking over a tenancy.

Immigration and deportation

Clearly, control on immigration and compulsory deportation may disrupt family life. In a number of cases the Strasbourg court has held that applicants have to demonstrate obstacles to establishing family life in their mother country in order for a refusal of admission by a state to be a violation of Art.8. The Convention does not guarantee any right to enter and remain in a country of which the applicant is not a national. Therefore Art.8 cannot invalidate immigration controls in themselves. In *Abdulaziz, Cabales and Balkandali v UK* (1985), the challenge was over immigration rules which disqualified men who had never met their spouses from lawfully settling in the UK (although women in the same position would be given indefinite leave to remain). The court held that:

> "... the duty imposed by Article 8 cannot be considered as extending to a general obligation on the part of a contracting state to respect the choice by married couples of the country of their matrimonial residence and to accept the non-national spouses for settlement in that country".

Further, states had a wide margin of appreciation in determining what steps should be taken to ensure compliance with the Convention. There was here no lack of respect for family life since the applicants had not shown there were obstacles to establishing family life in their own or their husbands' countries.

With regard to deportations the court may find a violation of the right to family life if the deportee has no real connection with the country to which he is to be sent or he has very firm links with the country expelling him (see *Nasri v France* (1995)). Short of that, the court normally accepts the state's judgment as for example in Court of Appeal decision in *R. (Mahmood) v Secretary of State for the Home Department* (2001).

The territorial scope of Art.8 had been extended by the judgment of the House of Lords in *R. (Razgar) v Secretary of State for the Home Department* which followed that in *Ullah and Do* (2004). The House held that the right respect for private life protected by Art.8 could be engaged by the foreseeable consequences for health of removal from the United Kingdom following an immigration decision. It was not the case that only Art.3 could be relied on to resist a removal decision by immigration authorities. The House emphasised that similar stringent tests would be applied when applications relied on Art.8 as on Art.3. It would frustrate the proper and necessary object of immigration control in the more advanced members states of the Council of Europe if illegal entrants requiring medical treatment could not, save in exceptional cases, be removed to the less-developed countries of the world where comparable medical facilities were not available. (See also *Bensaid v UK* (2001)).

Children

A number of cases have reviewed the rights of parents where public authorities, including the courts, are making decisions about removing children from the family. There may be violations of the provision if the parents are not given proper access to their children who are placed in care, or they do not have adequate input into the decisions over the children (see *Johansen v Norway* (1996); *W v UK* (1987); *McMichael v UK* (1995)).

Divorce, Separation, Access

Protecting family life implies also the right of married couples to separate. In *Airey v Ireland* (1979), lack of legal aid for court hearings was an infringement of this right in a situation where the wife had been subject to domestic violence. With regard to the position of the children of divorced parents in *Hendricks v Netherlands* (1983), the Commission declared:

> " . . . the right to respect for family life within the meaning of Article 8 of the Convention includes the right of [a] divorced parent, who is

deprived of custody following the break-up of marriage, to have access to or contact with his child".

However, the child's interests will be overriding and this may require a parent's access to be severely curtailed (*Whitear v UK* (1997)).

Home

This provision is closely related to that of family life and the two are somewhat overlapping. In addition it may overlap with Art.1 of the First Protocol (see below). In *Buckley v UK* (1996), the court considered that "Article 8 does not reasonably go so far as to allow individuals' preference as to their place of residence to override the general interest". The applicant, who was a gypsy, claimed that the removal of her caravan to an alternative site was a violation. The case concerned the right to respect for a "home" but the local authority's action was justified for environmental and economic reasons. In *Gillow v UK* (1986), the state's refusal to allow the applicants a licence to occupy their own home was a violation since it was disproportionate to the otherwise legitimate aim of protecting the economic well-being of Guernsey.

The home and the environment

Strasbourg has acknowledged that environmental pollution may be a violation of Art.8. In *Baggs, Powell and Raynor v UK* (1990), noise from Heathrow created a nuisance. The Commission noted:

> " . . . Considerable noise nuisance can undoubtedly affect the physical well being of a person and thus interfere with his private life. It may also deprive a person of the possibility of enjoying the amenities of his home".

However, the interference was not disproportionate to the legitimate aim of running the airport. By contrast, in *Guerra v Italy* (1998), pollution from a chemical factory a mile from the applicant's home provided grounds for a violation of Art.8, since the authorities had not provided relevant information about the risks to their health. There was a positive obligation to inform local people about health matters (see also *McGinley and Egan v UK* (1998)).

In *Lopez Ostra v Spain* (1994) the Strasbourg court decided that "severe environmental pollution" could violate Art.8. There was a retreat from this robust approach however in *Hatton v United Kingdom* (2003) that the applicants' Art.8 rights were not breached by a new Heathrow night flight scheme. The Grand Chamber of the Strasbourg Court reversed the earlier decision (*Hatton v UK*, 2002) which held that there were violations of Arts 8 and 13. The Grand Chamber said governments should consider the protection of the environment in acting within their margin of appreciation. However it also clearly indicated that environmental rights did not merit specific protection by the court.

In *Marcic v Thames Water Utilities* (2003) the House of Lords also emphasised the importance in environmental issues of public policy over the interests of individuals who are adversely affected by statutory provisions. In the Court of Appeal, Marcic had succeeded under the common law on the basis that sewage coming onto his land was an actionable nuisance. The House of Lords disagreed with this approach and held that it was for parliament and administrators not the courts to determine whether better sewers should have been built.

Correspondence

Most cases under this provision involve the rights of prisoners. In the landmark case of *Golder v UK* (1975), the court held that a prisoner's right to uncensored correspondence with a lawyer or a judicial body is a fundamental aspect of access to justice. With regard to other correspondence some interference may be justified under Art.8(2) (*Silver v UK* (1983)).

MARRIAGE

Article 12 is closely related to the provisions of Art.8. The difference is that it is very specific. It concentrates on the act of marriage and/or that of producing or adopting children. Article 8 on the other hand covers an ongoing situation. The different emphases of the provisions produce the somewhat anomalous position that a person might be accorded the right to marry but not to continue to live with his or her partner. This has been the case with prisoners (*Draper v UK* (1980)). In *R. v Secretary of State for the Home Department, Ex p. Mellor* (2001), Forbes J. held that the Convention placed no obligation on the State to facilitate a prisoner's artificial insemination of his wife. The applicant was a man serving life for murder who married a former member of the prison staff. The prisoner had argued that his right to found a family had neither been expressly removed by statute nor implicitly by reason of prison management and that his wife's right to found a family had been violated.

On the other hand, in 1985 the court held that a "family" is the outcome of a marriage and that "it is scarcely conceivable that the right to found a family should not encompass the right to live together". The distinction between the two Articles was explained by the Commission in *Cossey v UK*:

> "The distinction between Articles 8 and 12 must be seen essentially as a difference between protection under Article 8 of de facto family life irrespective of its legal status . . . and the right under Article 12 for two persons of opposite sex to be united in a formal legally recognised union".

Although national law must allow the fundamental right of persons to marry it may without violating the Convention refuse to allow them to divorce (*Johnston v Ireland* (1986)). This somewhat conservative stance was reflected in *Rees v UK* (1986), where the court stated:

> " . . . the right to marry guaranteed by Article 12 refers to the traditional marriage between persons of opposite biological sex. This appears also from the wording of the Article which makes it clear that Article 12 is mainly concerned to protect marriage as the basis of the family".

Art.5, Protocol No. 7, specifies that spouses within marriage should be treated equally "and in the event of its dissolution".

Homosexuals/transsexuals

See page 95. In another progressive move the government introduced in 2003 the Employment Equality (Sexual Orientation) Regulations which protect against direct and indirect discrimination on these grounds in employment. There are exceptions for a "genuine and determining occupational requirement" that must be applied in a "proportionate" way.

PROPERTY

Peaceful enjoyment of possessions

The right to peaceful enjoyment of possessions is often known as the right to property, protected by Protocol 1, Art.1. The right is available to persons and "legal persons". This substantive right may be restricted "in the public interest and subject to conditions provided for by law". The Article acknowledges the "right of a state to enforce such laws as it deems necessary to control the use of property in accordance with the general interest or to secure the payment of taxes or other contributions or penalties".

The scope of the Article is quite narrow, not surprisingly since the right to property raises controversial political and economic issues. In *Powell v UK* (1990) the court stated "This provision is mainly concerned with the arbitrary confiscation of property and does not in principle guarantee a right to the peaceful enjoyment of possession in a pleasant environment". However, there is some overlap between Art.8 and this Article. The court has emphasised that the test of necessity allowed in the Protocol is to be applied in the same manner as the justification in Art.8 (see *Gillow v UK* (1986)). Thus, for example, in relation to confiscation of property the state must show it has struck a fair balance between the rights of an individual and those of the community. This might be achieved by an adequate level of compensation.

What is meant by "possessions"?

In *Mellacher v Austria* (1989), the court held that the right to conclude tenancy agreements was part of the right to use real property and thus was an aspect of the possession of that property. The applicant had argued that the right to receive rents was a right to property separate from the right to use property. In this case Austria's policy of rent control, however, was within its margin of appreciation and there was no violation of the right to property. The deprivation of a licence may interfere with the right under the Protocol, although in *The Traktörer Aktiebolag v Sweden* (1991), the decision was made within permissible discretion. Similarly "goodwill" may be a possession. In *Van Marle v Netherlands* (1986), the court stated that the goodwill built up by the applicants "had in many respects the nature of a private right". There is, however, no protection afforded to the right to acquire property. Thus, when a mother was denied the right to will property to her daughter, the former, but not the latter, suffered a violation. "Possession" is quite a wide term and includes claims under private law as well as social security benefits.

One potentially controversial issue is the proceeds of pension funds. The Commission has held that the payment of contributions to a pension fund may in certain circumstances create a property right in a portion of such a fund and a modification of the pension rights under such a system could therefore in principle raise an issue under Protocol 1, Art.1. There is however no right to a pension under the Convention. In *Szrabjer and Clarke v UK* (1998), suspension of pensions to the applicants who had acquired rights under the state earnings-related pension scheme was a deprivation of property. It was however justified since they were being kept at the state's expense (see also p.128).

Interference with peaceful enjoyment of possessions

Under certain circumstances a state's actions over property, although technically not affecting ownership, may violate the right to peaceful enjoyment. This happened to property owners under a Stockholm City ordinance which allowed the city to expropriate any property it wanted (*Sporrong and Lonnroth v Sweden* (1982)).

Deprivation of possessions: the public and general interest

There have been a number of cases on the meaning of "the public interest" in this Article. The test seems to be more generous than that of "necessary in a democratic society" which is identified in other Articles. In *James v UK* (1986), the applicants complained that a statute which permitted some tenants to purchase the leasehold at below market value was a violation. The court disagreed:

> "The notion of 'public interest' is necessarily extensive. The court finding it natural that the margin of appreciation available to the legislature in implementing social and economic policies should be a wide one will respect the legislature's judgment as to what is 'in the public interest' even if the community at large has no direct use or enjoyment of the property".

In *Holy Monasteries v Greece* (1994), the issue of compensation was a relevant consideration in deciding whether there was a fair balance between the public interest and that of the property owners. The Greek government had passed a law which meant that disputed monastic land could be presumed to be state-owned. The court considered there was no guarantee of a right "to full compensation in all circumstances, since legitimate objectives of 'public interest' may call for reimbursement of less than the full market value". There was however a violation in this case where no compensation was given. In *Lithgow v UK* (1988), by contrast, the level of compensation was justified. The court saw no violation in the nationalisation of the aircraft and ship-building industries in itself and the level of compensation was consistent with the requirements of Art.1, Protocol 1: "The court will respect a national legislature's judgment in this respect unless manifestly without reasonable foundation".

Control on the use of property

This aspect of the Article may be at issue when the state attempts to secure the payment of taxes or fines. In *Mellacher v Austria* (1989), the court held that laws controlling the use of property "are especially common in the field of housing which in our modern societies is a central concern of social and economic policies". It is crucial that a fair balance between competing interests is struck. This test was applied and found satisfied in several cases where property was forfeited as a result of criminal or civil sanctions (see, for example, *Handyside v UK* (1976) and *Air Canada v UK* (1995)).

Taxes

The court has taken quite a lenient stance in relation to the state's taxation policy. In *National Provincial Building Society v UK* (1997), it upheld retrospective laws which amended a technical defect whereby applicants were attempting to recover tax they had paid.

Subject to conditions provided for by law

In *Hentrich v France* (1994), however, the French government had violated the Convention in relation to taxes. Regional authorities had not given individual property owners sufficient procedural protection in exercising their right to pre-empt a private property arrangement, which they had discretion to do by statute. The objective was to deter others from evading taxation but there was a disproportionate burden on the individual. Thus the court will consider whether the law is qualitatively fair. In *Tsomtsos v Greece* (1996), the state applied an inflexible system of awarding compensation for expropriation of property for the purpose of building a highway. In addition there was no judicial determination of the extent of loss. This was a violation.

7. POLITICAL AND RELIGIOUS RIGHTS

The rights preserved in Arts 9, 10 and 11 lie at the very heart of liberal democratic concepts. They express the Enlightenment values of tolerance, pluralism, liberty, free speech and freedom of action, which have a long tradition also in English law. They are generally regarded as fundamental to a just society for three reasons:

- (a) tolerance of others' views and their manifestations of them in speech or political action encourages healthy participation by citizens in current debates;
- (b) the free play of ideas creates a kind of market place out of which the truth will emerge;
- (c) the rights expressed in these Articles are considered a necessary way for individuals to express their personal autonomy and freedom to choose their way of life.

However, although these Articles do not create absolute rights, they are all qualified along similar lines. In addition, there is a certain amount of overlap between them and petitions often raise issues under more than one of the Articles.

"THOUGHT", "BELIEF", "CONSCIENCE", "RELIGION"

There are two aspects to Art.9: the right to hold a belief, etc., and the right to manifest it in some way. The first is absolute: there is no question of qualifying rights to thought itself. The second aspect however might involve impinging on the susceptibilities of others or have undesirable social effects, and is therefore a qualified right. Most cases involve manifestations of belief. Like Arts 10 and 11, this Article is subject to qualifications, but unlike the others it does not permit restrictions on the grounds of "national security". Cases raised under Art.9 may also involve potential violations of Art.10 or other Articles. These are usually investigated first.

What is meant by "thought", etc.?

A broad range of beliefs or religions falls within the scope of the Article. These include pacifism (*Arrowsmith v UK* (1978)), veganism (*H v UK* (1991)), druidism (*Chappell v UK* (1968)) and cults (*Church of X v UK* (1969)) as well as mainstream religions. The court stated in *Kokkinakis v Greece* (1993), that Art.9:

> "... is in its religious dimension, one of the most vital elements that go to make up the identity of believers and of their conception of life, but it is also a precious asset for atheists, agnostics, sceptics and the unconcerned".

On the other hand, there is a distinction drawn between personal belief and some political views. Thus, the concept of a political prisoner is not accepted. In *McFeely and Others v UK* (1980), it was held that freedom to manifest belief does not include the right of an IRA prisoner to wear his own clothes in prison.

Who may exercise the right?

As well as individuals the rights in Art.9 may be exercised by organisations (*Chappell v UK* (1968)). In *Church of X v UK* (1969), however, the Commission indicated that it might be difficult for an organisation to demonstrate a violation of its rights.

Worship, teaching, practice, observance

An act may not be protected if the court holds that it is not a "manifestation" but is "influenced" by it. This is illustrated by *Arrowsmith v UK* (1978), where the applicant alleged that her conviction for distributing pacifist leaflets to soldiers was a violation of her freedom of conscience and belief. Although pacifism was a belief protected by Art.9 the court held that her actions were not a manifestation of it (Art.10 was not violated because the state had a legitimate interest in national security). Again, in *Kalac v Turkey* (1996), the court found no violation in removing a soldier from the military because of his conduct and attitude rather than the manifestation of his religious belief.

State religion

In *Darby v Sweden* (1990), an applicant (a Finn working in Sweden) claimed a violation in requiring him to contribute to the

Lutheran church of Sweden. Registered residents of Sweden could claim exemption. There was a violation of his right to peaceful enjoyment of property (Art.1, Protocol 1) and Art.14 but it was considered unnecessary to investigate whether there was a violation of Art.9.

Conscientious objectors

The court has been cautious in applying the Article to this group. The issue is examined along with Art.4(3)(b) banning "Forced or compulsory labour" but permitting alternative service for conscientious objectors to military service. In a number of cases, including *Autio v Finland* (1991), Strasbourg has decided that Art.9 does not entitle conscientious objectors to claim exemption from military service.

Employment and religious discrimination

Similarly, the court is slow to accept the concept of indirect discrimination on religious grounds. In *Stedman v UK* (1997), an application was held inadmissible where it was claimed that a requirement that a Christian should work on Sundays breached her rights under Art.9: "Ms Stedman was dismissed for failing to agree to work certain hours rather than for her religious beliefs as such and was free to resign and did in effect resign from her employment". She refused to accept the new contract. The importance attached to contractual obligations was evidenced also in *Ahmad v UK* (1981), where the applicant teacher, who was a devout Muslim, petitioned on the grounds that his request to be allowed to go to the Mosque for Friday prayer was refused by the local education authority. The Commission considered that there was no violation since a person "may, in the exercise of his freedom to manifest his religion, have to take into account his particular professional or contractual position".

These two cases show the limitations of the impact of the Human Rights Act. As Britain becomes more and more heterogeneous in population and increasing importance is attached to multi-culturalism, difficult questions of conflicts of interests such as that in *Ahmad* are posed. It could be argued that insofar as discrimination on religious grounds impacts particularly on a racial group it is prohibited by existing UK race relations legislation. However, religious groups as such, for example Rastafarians, are not so protected. The Employment Equality

(Religion or Belief) Regulations 2003 introduced in Britain provisions against both direct and indirect discrimination in employment on these grounds. There are exceptions where being of a particular religion or belief can be "a genuine and determining occupational requirement" which must be applied in a way which is "proportionate".

Language

In the *Belgian Linguistic Case* (1968), the court rejected the argument that because "thought" and language are so clearly connected any restrictions by the state on the exercise of minority languages are a violation of Art.9.

Restrictions

Any acceptable restriction to the manifestation of a belief must be in accordance with law, pursuing a legitimate aim as set out in Art.9(2) and necessary and proportionate. The issue was addressed in *Kokkinakis v Greece* where two Jehovah's Witnesses had been convicted of proselytism. The court held that attempting to convert others was a manifestation within the Article, that the state's limitation on this was lawful, and had the legitimate aim of the protection of the rights and freedoms of others. There was a violation of Art.9 however, in that the prosecution was not justified by a pressing need. The law was therefore disproportionate.

Relationship with Article 10

The relationship between the two Articles has come up particularly over the question of blasphemy, which in England is a law uniquely protecting the Christian religion. In *Gay News and Lemon v UK* (1982), the Commission found that a private prosecution arising out of the law on blasphemy did not breach Art.10, the legitimate purpose at stake was the protection of the rights of others. Again this was the position taken in *Wingrove v UK* (1994), where a video, "Visions of Ecstasy", was refused a classification on the basis that it infringed the criminal law of blasphemy. The Court points out that:

> "the English law of blasphemy does not prohibit the expression, in any form, of views hostile to the Christian religion. Nor can it be said that opinions which are offensive to Christians necessarily fall

within its ambit ... It is the manner in which views are advocated rather than the views themselves which the law seeks to control".

There was no violation of Art.10. On the other hand, the Commission has not accepted that there is a violation of Art.9 in the failure of English blasphemy law to protect Muslims (*Choudhury v UK* (1991)). However, in a pluralist society such as Britain it is arguable that a criminal law which protects just one religion is not acceptable. Human rights law as presently expressed in the cases does not seek to redress this anomaly. One solution is to criminalise attacks on all religions. Two attempts to make incitement to religious hatred a criminal offence were voted down by the House of Lords in December 2001 when the Home Secretary tried to incorporate the proposed offence into anti-terrorism legislation. In July 2004 it was announced that the measure would be resubmitted to the Lords. The Government proposes to extend the law of incitement to racial hatred to those attacked because of their religion. Opposition to the proposal is likely from secularists who fear that such a measure may be used to muzzle those who simply criticise religion.

Prisoners

In a number of cases prisoners have claimed they have not been free to practice their beliefs in prison. They have not usually been successful. The concept of political prisoner is not accepted. In *McFeely and Others v UK* (1980), it was held that freedom to manifest belief does not include the right of a prisoner to wear his own clothes in prison.

FREEDOM OF EXPRESSION

The right to freedom of expression is protected by all the most significant international human rights instruments, and the European Court of Human Rights in particular has developed a great deal of case law on this area. Some of the most significant findings against the UK have involved violations of this Article, *e.g. Sunday Times v UK* (1979), which led to a change in the laws on contempt. English law does recognise that people are generally free to express themselves and share information in any way they please, subject only to specific legal restraints. It is anticipated that application of Art.10 will have a liberalising effect on English law. To take one example, the House of Lords in *Reynolds v Times Newspapers* (1999), did not acknowledge that in relation to defamation proceedings politicians should be treated differently from private individuals. It rejected a defence argument that a new category of qualified privilege, "political information", should be created. Instead the House developed the existing common law in giving qualified privilege wherever, in the specific circumstances of the case, it is in the public interest for the statement to be communicated to the public. By contrast, the Strasbourg court has recognised that the position of a politician is different from that of a private individual (see *Lingens v Austria* (1986)). This is an evolving area and the courts have acknowledged that the public have an interest in the promotion of a free and vigorous press. Journalists have correspondingly to act responsibly, (see *Loutchansky v Times Newspapers Ltd* (No.2) (2001)).

Meaning of "expression"

The term "expression" is not fully defined. It includes artistic works (*Muller and Others v Switzerland* (1988)), as well as publications, video, films, and also conduct intending to convey ideas or information (*Hashman and Harrup v UK* (2000)).

Political expression

The objective of Art.10 is to allow the free play of political ideas since this is regarded as healthy for democracy. However states may legitimately interfere with the right if other interests require it and the response is proportionate.

In *Bowman v UK* (1998), the applicant had been prosecuted for distributing news on abortion and embryo experimentation which was in breach of the requirements on election expenses under the Representation of the People Act 1983. Since the "aim of influencing others who are themselves responsible for their actions is an essential and legitimate aspect of the exercise of freedom of expression and opinion, in political and other matters", this was a violation of Art.10.

In *Ahmed and Others v UK* (1999), the restrictions on the political activities of certain ranks of local government officers was not a disproportionate interference with their rights under Arts 10 and 11. The regulations were justified by the pressing social need to uphold political neutrality of public officials.

In R. *(Persey) v Secretary of State for the Environment, Food and Rural Affairs* (2002) the claimants sought judicial review of the government's decision to hold in private an inquiry into the lessons learnt from the 2001 foot and mouth disease outbreak. They argued that such an inquiry was essential to restore public confidence, and that it was a violation of their right to freedom of expression to hold the inquiry sessions in private. The Divisional Court held that there was no presumption that inquiries would be held in public and it was a political decision for the Secretary of State whether to make the sessions public. The decision not to hold the sessions in public was not irrational. Article 10 did not require that such inquiries be held in public and so was not violated by not doing so. Article 10 was engaged where the authorities of a state refused entry to an individual solely to prevent his expression of opinion within its territory. However, the Court of Appeal held in R. *(Farrakhan) v Secretary of State for the Home Department* (2002) that the Home Office's refusal to relax the ban on the leader of the Nation of Islam struck a proportionate balance between the legitimate aims of the prevention of disorder and freedom of expression to the extent to which that was in play on the facts of the case.

The scope of Art.10(2) was reviewed by the House of Lords in R. *v Shayler* (2002). The argument that the Official Secrets Act 1989 was incompatible with Art.10 was rejected since the restrictions imposed by the Act were proportionate and pursued a legitimate aim The objective of preserving secrecy of intelligence and military operations was sanctioned by previous Strasbourg cases.

Protest

Peaceful political protest may be protected. In *Steel v UK* (1999), the court held that there was a violation of right to freedom of expression of some of the demonstrators when peaceful protesters were detained under the Public Order Act 1986 and bound over to keep the peace. They had been handing out leaflets against weapon sales (see also *Hashman and Harrup v UK* (2000)). *Steel* is a significant case because the court also took the view that the actions of two other demonstrators constituted "expression" even though they were disrupting the activities of others, and in their case the legal action taken against them was disproportionate. These decisions show the close connection between Arts 10 and 11. The court's decision follows similar reasoning to that in *Redmond-Bate v DPP* (1999), where a woman preacher, whose words it was feared would lead to others being incited, was arrested. The Divisional Court held that the freedom of speech which was protected by the ECHR, applied to "the irritating, the contentious, the heretical, the unwelcome and the provocative provided it did not tend to provoke violence". The arrest was not lawful.

Obscenity

Freedom of expression may mean that words may cause offence to others. The words of the Divisional Court in *Redmond-Bate* mirror those of the Strasbourg Court in *Handyside v UK* (1976), which acknowledged the need to protect expressions that "offend, shock or disturb the state or any sector of the population. Such are the demands of that pluralism, tolerance and broadmindedness without which there is no democratic society". However, the conviction of a publisher or a sexually explicit book for schoolchildren was within the state's margin of appreciation, for the "protection of morals". In other cases religious sensibilities may be rightfully protected even though this might limit the exercise of artistic freedom. Thus in *Wingrove v UK* (1996), there was no violation of Art.10 where the respective governments prohibited the exhibition of films that showed disrespectful images of some Christian figures.

Freedom of the press

Contempt

The leading case is *Sunday Times v UK* (1979), where the court held that the granting of an injunction restraining the publication of details of the manufacturers' procedures in testing Thalidomide was a violation of Art.10. It was "prescribed by law", namely the common law, but had failed to satisfy the "pressing social need" test and was not proportionate. The court considered that the families affected by the scandal of Thalidomide production had a vital interest in knowing all the underlying facts and the various possible solutions. They could be deprived of this information, which was crucially important for them, only if it appeared absolutely certain that its diffusion would have presented a threat to the "authority of the judiciary". In addition the public had a right to receive information on the issue.

Defamation

In *Linens v Austria* (1986), the court held that successful private defamation actions brought by prominent politicians were a violation of Art.10. Its arguments were set clearly in a liberal democratic tradition:

> "Freedom of the press . . . affords the public one of the best means of discovering and forming an opinion of the ideas and attitudes of political leaders. More generally freedom of political debate is at the very core of the concept of a democratic society which prevails throughout the Convention".

Interestingly, the Court criticised the Austrian defamation law for placing the burden of proof on the defendant to establish the truth of his statement. English law of defamation places the burden of proof on the defence. The English law came up for criticism in *Tolstoy-Miloslavsky v UK* (1995). This concerned £1.5m libel damages, which were so high as to be a breach of Art.10. They were not necessary in a democratic society.

Confidentiality and injunctions

Two joined cases arising out of the *Spycatcher* saga reached the court, namely *Observer and Guardian v UK* (1991) and *Sunday Times v UK* (1991). The court showed here its deference to the concept of national security, which muted its criticisms of the decisions of the English courts. It found that the temporary injunction fell within the state's margin of appreciation in assessing the possible threat to national security. However, the continuation of the injunction after the material was in the public domain because of overseas publication was a violation of Art.10. In *Venables v News Group Newspapers Ltd* (2001) Dame Elizabeth Butler-Sloss P., in The Family Division, granted permanent injunctions restraining publication of information on the identity of the killers of James Bulger. Publication would risk their rights under Arts 2 and 3. Section 12 of the Human Rights Act will make it more difficult for a pre-trial injunction to be awarded against the press.

Journalists' sources

The gap between the protection afforded to Press freedom under English law and the requirements of Art.10 was further illustrated in *Goodwin v UK* (1996). The court found a violation Art.10

where the public authority imposed on a journalist both an injunction against the publication of an article and an order to disclose the sources of his information. Significantly, the protection of the commercial interests of the company was a legitimate aim but the measures to achieve them were disproportionate. The House of Lords again considered disclosure of journalists' sources in *Ashworth Hospital Authority v MGN* (2002), a case concerning the treatment of Ian Brody, the Moors Murderer. It ordered disclosure. The ECtHR found a violation of Art.10 in *De Haes and Gijsels v Belgium* (1997) where journalists suffered a penalty for publishing an article critical of a decision on the custody of a child (awarded to man convicted of incest). The suggestion was that the judges acted with political bias.

Commercial interests

In *Ashdown v Telegraph Group* (2001), for example, Sir Andrew Morritt V.-C. in the Chancery Division held that where a copyright infringer could not make out one of the statutory exceptions or defences under the Copyright Designs and Patents Act 1988, it was not open to him to defend proceedings on the basis that the 1988 Act restricted the right to freedom of expression further than was necessary in a democratic society and thus was contrary to Art.10(2). There are very few Strasbourg cases claiming violations of Art.10 in the context of commercial enterprises, perhaps suggesting that national law has proved adequate in this area. In *Markt Intern GmbH and Klaus Beerman v Germany* (1990), the publishers of a trade publication criticising commercial activities of a large firm petitioned against a domestic court decision curtailing further publication. The court found no violation. Thus, commercial information is a protected interest. The growing importance of the protection of "whistleblowers", now subject to legislation, may well raise Art.10 issues.

Broadcasting

Broadcast licensing

The Convention expressly gives states power to license broadcasting, television or cinema enterprises (Art.10(1)). However, the court has held that states must be able to justify licensing requirements in the light of the purposes of the Article as a whole. In *Informationsverein Lentia v Austria* (1993) and *Radio ABC v Austria* (1997), the applicants contested the government's decision to deny them licences to broadcast. They were effectively challenging a monopoly enjoyed by Austrian State broadcasting. The court found that State monopolies over broadcasting imposed the greatest restrictions on pluralism in expression and thus could only be justified by pressing social need, which had not been demonstrated. Government interference with the reception of broadcasts was at issue in *Groppera Radio v Switzerland* (1990), in which the applicants challenged a prohibition on retransmission by cable of programmes originally broadcast from Italy. The court held that the government ban was "necessary in order to prevent evasion of the law" and was not a form of censorship. However, the Swiss State restrictions were found to have exceeded what was necessary in a democratic society in *Autronic v Switzerland* (1990), which concerned a television company refused permission to broadcast uncoded television programmes received from a Soviet satellite, in the absence of Soviet consent. Because the broadcasts were intended for general public use and would not give away secret information, the restrictions exceeded the state's margin of appreciation.

The difficulty of applying the test of whether any restriction on freedom of expression is "necessary in a democratic society" was illustrated in the controversial decision of the House of Lords in *R. (Prolife Alliance) v BBC* (2003). Reversing the Court of Appeal, it held (Lord Scott dissenting) that the BBC and other broadcasters were entitled to refuse to broadcast a party election broadcast by the Prolife Alliance on the ground that it was offensive to public feeling.

Extremism

Racist expressions

Article 10(2) lists the protection of others as a legitimate interest. Barriers to extremist activity are also set out in Art.17:

> "Nothing in this Convention may be interpreted as implying for any state, group or person any right to engage in any activity or perform any act aimed at the destruction of the rights and freedoms set forth herein or at their limitation to a greater extent than is provided for in the Convention".

There are a number of cases where Art.17 has been held to justify prosecuting racists for publishing or distributing racist material (see, for example, *Kuhnen v Germany* (1988)). Merely broadcasting views of self-proclaimed racists should not be criminalised, however. Thus, there was a violation in *Jersild v Denmark* (1994) where a journalist was prosecuted for putting out a television documentary publicising views of racists. The court stated: "News reporting based on interviews, whether edited or not, constituted one of the most important means whereby the press is able to play its vital role as a public watchdog". The conviction was disproportionate.

Access to information

Does the Article protect "freedom of information"?

The "culture of secrecy" has been condemned as a British disease, although the Data Protection Acts 1984 and 1998 and the Freedom of Information Act 2000 make significant inroads into this secrecy. UK governments and authorities that wish to protect information may find some comfort in the decision in *Leander v Sweden* (1987). The Swedish government had refused to give his file to an applicant they had turned down for a job on security grounds. The court did not accept this was a violation, partly on the grounds that the "freedom to receive information" requirement in Art.10 "prohibits a government from restricting a person from receiving information that others wish or may be willing to impart to him". The Article did not confer on an individual a right of access to a register containing information on his personal position, nor did it embody an obligation on the government to impart such information to the individual. In *Gaskin v UK* (1989) the UK government's refusal to grant a young man access to files relating to his time in care did not violate Art.10, though Art.8 was violated.

Both the right to impart and the right to have access to information about the availability of abortions abroad were at issue in *Open Door Counselling and Dublin Well Woman v Ireland* (1992). An injunction preventing the two companies from giving such information to pregnant women as part of counselling services was overturned. The court noted the sweeping nature of the injunction, the availability of such information from other sources and the lack of any prohibition against women going abroad to have an abortion.

The Freedom of Information Act 2000 comes into force on New Years Day 2005. It confers two statutory rights on anyone regardless of age, nationality or location. The first is to be told whether a public authority holds information and the second is to have that information communicated to them. The Act applies to central and local government, the National Health Service, police and armed forces, the education sector and other public bodies. Request for information must be made in writing stating what information is required and giving the applicant's name and address. Exemptions are made for information that is embargoed for future release, and for information relating to the Security Service, the Secret Intelligence Service, the Government Communications Headquarters, the special forces, the national criminal intelligence service and a range of tribunals and security vetting panels. Public authorities will be required to draw up a publication scheme for the production, maintenance and disclosure of information they hold. Private organisations which carry out public functions may also be required to draw up schemes and open their archives.

Employment

Public sector

In a number of cases involving public sector employees the court has clearly attached much importance to the right to freedom of expression. Several have involved the Federal Republic of Germany's policy of requiring all civil servants to swear allegiance to the Constitution. In the 1986 cases (*Kosiek v Federal Republic of Germany and Glasenapp v Federal Republic of Germany*) two probationary teachers, one a far left-wing sympathiser, the other a far right-winger, were denied permanent appointments. The court found there was no violation of Art.10. By contrast, the ILO found the government in violation of its obligations under the ILO Discrimination (Employment and Occupation) Convention 1958. Some nine years later, following Germany's reunification, the court changed its stance. The German government had violated Art.10 in dismissing a teacher because she was a member of the German Communist Party (*Vogt v Germany* (1995)).

FREEDOM OF ASSEMBLY AND ASSOCIATION

It is sometimes said that the Convention protects only classical liberal individual rights. This is not so. Protection is afforded to rights of assembly and association, which are essentially collective rights. Article 11, however, inevitably involves a balance of conflicting interests. Citizens may wish on the one hand to be free from public disorder in their everyday lives and on the other to propagate ideas in a way which will attract attention, by pickets, demonstration or meetings. In addition, rights to assemble may offend the right to property. Since traditionally there have been no entrenched legal rights to assembly or associate, the central problem in this area has been to preserve public order, in part on the basis that such order is vital for the continuation of basic freedoms, and for the efficient functioning of the state and its economic and social infrastructure.

The common law background

The historic pattern in English law has been that parliament legislates to deal with perceived public order problems arising from particular demonstrations or public assemblies. These laws then remain on the statute book to apply more generally. Each statute has placed increasing restrictions on the rights to demonstrate and picket. The Public Order Act 1936 was passed in the wake of the Mosleyite riots of the early 1930s, the Public Order Act 1986 in the wake of the miners' strike and anti-nuclear demonstrations and the Criminal Justice and Public Order Act 1994 after the activities of the new age travellers and hunt saboteurs. The law is not concerned with the source of the disorder so football hooligans and poll tax demonstrators are subject to the same restrictions. The government was asked to include the "right to demonstrate" in the provisions of the 1986 Act but confined itself to "reminding" the police of this in Home Office circulars.

To some extent the importance of Art.11 has been overshadowed by the increasingly liberal interpretation given to Art.10. Thus in *Steel v UK* (1998) and *Hashman and Harrup v UK* (2000), the activities of the anti-hunt activists were seen as manifestations of expression rather than assembly. The close association of these two Articles underlies their joint importance in upholding the political and social values of a democratic society. The qualifications to the Article are concerned in similar terms to those of Arts 8, 9 and 10, except for the inclusion of permissible and lawful restrictions on the exercise of these rights by members of the armed forces, of the police or of the administration of the state. The Article protects two specific activities, freedom of peaceful assembly and freedom of association with others.

Peaceful assembly

Such gatherings cover a fairly broad scope of activities: "as such this right covers both private meetings and meetings in public thoroughfares".

Prior authorisation and bans

A procedure set up by the authorities for prior authorisation or bans for public assemblies was not necessarily a breach of Art.11 (App. No. 8191/78). The principle established in English common law that a peaceful assembly might be restricted if it could provoke violence in others (see *O'Kelly v Harvey* (1883)) may be reassessed in applying the Human Rights Act. The Commission has declared that:

> "The right to freedom of peaceful assembly is secured to everyone who has the intention of organising a peaceful demonstration—the possibility of violent counter-demonstrations, or the possibility of extremists with violent intentions, not members of the organising association, joining the demonstration cannot as such take away that right".

However, the Commission stated that the government was acting within its margin of appreciation in banning all public demonstrations where there was a reasonable likelihood of a real threat to public safety and order. Similarly, although the authorities have an obligation to protect citizens exercising the right of peaceful protest, "they cannot guarantee this absolutely and they have a wide discretion in the choice of means to be used". In this area the obligation they enter into under Art.11 of the Convention is an obligation as to measures to be taken and not as to results to be achieved (*Platform Artze für das Leben v Austria* (1988)).

Sanctions against demonstrators

The authorities may breach Art.11 if they take too heavy-handed an approach to demonstrators. Such measures will have to pass the test of proportionality and be necessary in a democratic society (see *Ezelin v France* (1991)).

The right to association

The Commission explained in *Young, James and Webster v UK* (1979), that the "term 'association' presupposes a voluntary grouping for a common goal".

Voluntary grouping and trade unions

The meaning of voluntary has come in for some scrutiny in a trade union context. The Article refers specifically to the right to join a trade union but the words "right not to join a trade union" had been omitted from the original draft of the Convention. It is accepted that this arose from the acknowledgement of the practice of the "closed shop" then in operation in the UK. Under this system and prevailing legislation, if employers and recognised unions agreed that all workers should be in a specific trade union the dismissal of a worker for refusing to join was lawful (there were some recognised exceptions for grounds of conscience.) The law has now been changed. The approach of the Commission and the court to the question of the closed shop has been criticised by some trade union supporters as restrictive. The issue is however quite complex.

In *Young, James and Webster v UK* (1981), the court found a violation in that the law allowed the dismissal of a worker who was already in employment (it was a newly negotiated closed shop agreement). The applicants should not be compelled to join a trade union in order to keep their jobs but it was significant that this was an issue of continued employment:

> "The situation facing the applicants clearly runs counter to the concept of freedom of association in its negative sense. Assuming that Article 11 does not guarantee the negative aspect of that freedom on the same footing as the positive aspect, compulsion to join a particular trade union may not always be contrary to the Convention. However a threat of dismissal involving loss of livelihood is a most serious form of compulsion, and, in the present instance, it was directed against persons engaged by British Rail before the introduction of any obligation to join a trade union".

By contrast, in *Sibson v UK* (1993) there was no violation of Art.11 after an employer transferred a worker to another place of work because he left one union to join another and other workers would not accept him. There was no risk to his job.

Trade union rights

The court has limited its interpretation of the protection of trade unions to the right to form and to join. This does not include the right to strike (*Schmidt and Dahlstrom v Sweden* (1976)), where the court declined to give an unqualified approval to the right although it acknowledged it was "without any doubt one of the most important means" whereby trade unions can defend their interests. It stated that the right, "which is not expressly enshrined in article 11, may be subject under national law to regulation ... ". The court referred to the European Social Charter, which protects the right to strike and allows some qualifications. The sort of regulation the court accepts is given in the decision in *NATFHE v UK* (1998), where it found no violation of Art.11 in the statutory requirement to give to an employer the names of trade union members before strike action was begun. The court did not see that Art.11 guarantees the right to consult with any particular union (*National Union of Belgian Police* (1975)), nor have a collective agreement concluded (*Swedish Engine Drivers Union* (1976)), nor create the right to join a particular union in certain circumstances (*Cheall v UK* (1985). The Commission has acknowledged also that the internal affairs of trade unions should be free from state interference.

A recent decision has demonstrated that the ECHR is capable of defending collective as well as individual rights. In *Wilson v UK, Palmer v UK* (2002) the court held that the United Kingdom had failed in its positive obligation to secure the enjoyment of rights under Art.11. Individuals were entitled not only to join trade unions but also to enjoy some minimum rights as a consequence. There was a violation of Art.11 since the national legislation allowed employers to refuse pay rises to union members who refused to relinquish their union membership and engage in individual rather than collective bargaining.

Prisoners

A group of prisoners failed in their claim that solitary confinement violated their right of association *McFeeley v UK* (1980).

Qualifications on Article 11

Uniquely, Art.11 allows states to apply restrictions on three groups: the armed forces, the police and civil servants. Their application was reviewed in *Council of Civil Service Unions and*

Others v UK (1987). Workers at the Government Communication Headquarters were refused the right to join a trade union.

Common goal

Trade unions, according to the Commission and the court, exhibit the "common goal" requirement. However, the position of professional associations is less clear. There, compulsory membership may be acceptable but the case law suggests such bodies fulfil public law regulatory functions rather than being voluntary "associations" (*Le Compte, van Leuvan and de Meyere v Belgium* (1981)). The Commission rejected the complaint in *Council of Civil Service Unions and Others v UK* (1987) as ill founded. There had been an interference with Art.11 rights but since the petitioners fell within the definition of "members of the administration of the state" it was not an association. Furthermore, in the case of national security a wide margin of appreciation was allowed. The ILO held the UK was in breach of the relevant Articles of the International Labour Convention on Freedom of Association.

The right to free elections

By Art.3, Protocol 1, the High Contracting Parties undertook to hold free elections at reasonable intervals by secret ballot, under conditions which would ensure the free expression of the people's opinion in the choice of the legislature. Clearly this is not an individual freedom but a positive obligation imposed on the state. The importance of this Article was emphasised by the Commission in the *Greek Case* (1969), when it stated: "The existence of a representative legislature, elected at reasonable intervals, is the basis of a democratic society". The right to vote is only implied in the Article. As the court made clear in *Mathieu-Mohin and Clerfayt v Belgium* (1987), states enjoy a considerable margin of appreciation and the court will only interfere if the essence of the protected rights is interfered with.

In *R. v Secretary of State for the Home Department, Ex p. Pearson* (2001), the Administrative Court upheld the disenfranchising of convicted prisoners, since Parliament had decided they had forfeited their right to a say in the way the country was governed. The Strasbourg Court ruled in *Hirsk v UK* (2004) that the blanket denial to convict prisoners of the right to vote was a violation of their Convention rights (see p.45).

8. SOCIAL RIGHTS—DISCRIMINATION

The Convention contains few explicit references to social rights. Like economic rights—such as the right to a job—these involve political decisions about the allocation of resources and are therefore more controversial. Of course, some social and economic rights are referred to, specifically those involving family life and the right to peaceful enjoyment of possessions. The right to join a trade union is also of course a social and economic right. One specific social right which is protected is that to education. It could be argued that the right to equal treatment, or freedom from discrimination, is a basic requirement of a liberal society. In that sense it is a social, political and economic right. The principle of equality at one level means that everyone should be treated equally before the law. In this formal aspect the Convention rights are available to all individuals. However, with regard to the social and economic aspect of equality, that is that goods and benefits should be equally distributed, the Convention is less sure-footed. Some distinctions are acceptable. The issue is whether these fall into the area of discrimination which is prohibited.

The Convention does not as yet provide a freestanding right not to be discriminated against but Art.14 required that the rights that are set out in the Convention should be secured without discrimination on a wide range of grounds. Some reference has been made to this in discussing substantive rights and in this chapter we look more closely at the application of Art.14.

RIGHT TO EDUCATION

The concern about resources is evidenced in the UK's reservation to Protocol 1, Art.2. The Article specifies that "no person shall be denied the right to education". The UK accepts "only so far as it is compatible with the provision of efficient instruction and training and the avoidance of unreasonable public expenditure" (*Campbell and Cosans v UK* (1982)).

A negative right

Significantly, the requirement is that the State shall not deny rather than it should positively guarantee or respect the right.

The burden is on the individual to prove interference, not the State to defend non-provision. The Article gives the State discretion on the scope of its provision since it refers to "the exercise of any functions which it assumed in relation to education and to teaching". In *Douglas v North Tyneside Metropolitan Borough Council* (2003) the Court of Appeal explored the content of the right to education stating the higher education could be protected under the Convention. It stressed, however, that extending the scope of education did not mean additional obligations on governments.

Pluralism

The second sentence of the Protocol requires the State to "respect the right of parents to ensure such education and teaching in conformity with their own religious and philosophical convictions". In *Campbell and Cosans v UK* (1982), the court accepted that petitioners had established a violation by the State in relation to the use of corporal punishment in schools and the suspension of the child. It thus took a broad view of education to encompass "the development and moulding of the character and mental powers of the pupils". The "philosophical convictions" which were not respected related to:

> " . . . a weighty and substantial aspect of human life and behaviour, namely the integrity of the person, the propriety or otherwise of the infliction of corporal punishment and the exclusion of the distress which the risk of such punishment entails".

The right of the suspended child had been violated, "the right set out in the second sentence being an adjunct of the fundamental right to education".

Minority languages

In the *Belgian Linguistic Case (No.2)* (1968), the court held that the Article did not entitle French-speaking residents living in the Flemish-speaking part of Belgium to be educated in French:

> "The negative formulation indicates . . . that the contracting Parties do not recognise such a right to education as would require them to establish at their own expense, or to subsidise, education of any particular type or at any particular level".

Secondary and tertiary education

The Article is primarily concerned with elementary education. There is no obligation to ensure that certain groups such as prisoners or foreigners are given access to more specialised education such as university education. Restriction of access is allowed.

Home/private education

Both of these are acceptable. Although the State is not required to fund them it may regulate them (*Family H v UK* (1984)).

Sex education

In *Kjeldsen, Busk Madsen and Pedersen v Denmark* (1976), the parents of schoolchildren protested about the inclusion of sex education. The court said that the State:

> " . . . must take care that information of knowledge included in the curriculum is conveyed in an objective, critical and pluralistic manner. The state is forbidden to pursue an aim of indoctrination that might be considered as not respecting parents' religious and philosophical convictions."

The State could not avoid this responsibility by reference to the legality of private schools. If so it would lead to the position that only the rights of wealthy parents were "respected". In this instance the petition failed because the lessons imparted information not indoctrination.

DISCRIMINATION

Article 14 contains a wide, not exhaustive range of prohibited grounds of discrimination, "such as sex, race, colour, language, religion, political or other opinion, national or social origin, association with a national minority, property, birth or other status". The subject matter of the claim has to fall within one of the Articles of the Convention. So if, for example, the claim is in discrimination of access to civil service employment it will fail. This access is not a guaranteed right. However, there is no need for a finding of a violation of that provision in order for Art.14 to be engaged. Most cases, however, do involve allegations of both violations. The court attaches more importance to the substantive right and if a finding of a violation is made will not usually go on to consider the discrimination claim (*Smith and Grady v UK* (2000)). To establish differential treatment, the applicant must show that he or she has been less favourably treated than others in a similar or analogous situation.

Discrimination

In *Ghaidan v Godin-Mendoza* (2004) the House of Lords upheld a decision of the Court of Appeal that an Act which allowed the spouse of a protected tenant to succeed to the tenancy on the tenant's death should be read so that the word "spouse" included a homosexual partner. The House held it was necessary and possible to read the Act in this way in order to give effect to the homosexual partner's Convention right not to be discriminated against and his right to family life. The strained reading of the provision was preferable to making a declaration of incompatibility, which was the alternative course the court could have taken. Lord Steyn's speech contains a useful appendix listing declarations of incompatibility made by the courts since the Human Rights Act became law, and cases in which statutes have been (re)–construed in the light of the Act. The case is notable for a spirited dissent by Lord Millett, who observed that the word "spouse" meant a party to a lawful marriage and necessarily implied a person of the opposite sex. He said: "Marriage is the lawful union of a man and a woman. It is a legal relationship between persons of the opposite sex. A man's spouse must be a woman; a woman's spouse must be a man. This is of the very essence of the relationship, which need not be loving, sexual, stable, faithful, long-lasting, or contented."

The impact of the Human Rights Act on social benefits is seen in *R. (Hooper) v Secretary of State for Work and Pensions* (2003). The Court of Appeal held that the non-availability of widows' benefits for widowers under the Social Security Contributions and Benefits Act 1992 was contrary to Arts 14 and 16. It held that the Human Rights Act allowed extra statutory payment to be made to the claimants. It added "the Human Rights Act introduces a presumption into the principle of statutory interpretation that Parliament does not intend legislation to infringe the Convention. It follows that neither section 6(2) nor section 6(2)(b) affords the Secretary of State a defence to the claim that by failing to make extra-statutory payments to the claimants he infringed Article 14 of the Convention."

Racial discrimination

In its public statement on the case of *East African Asians v UK* (1973), the Commission stated that actions which are racially motivated may be a violation of Art.3 even though the subject matter of the discrimination is not a right articulated in the Convention. Here the UK had refused entrance to British passport holders. There is no guarantee in the Convention of the right to immigration. Another example of a robust approach to racial discrimination is *Abdulaziz, Cabales and Balkandali v UK* (1985). There was no violation of Art.8 since non-national spouses had no right to settled under the Convention, but there was a violation of Art.14:

> "The notion of discrimination within the meaning of Article 14 includes in general cases where a person or group is treated, without proper justification, less favourably than another, even though the more favourable treatment is not called for by the Convention".

Discrimination allowed

In *Ireland v UK* (1978), the petitioners claimed that anti-terrorist legislation discriminated against the Catholic community. This appeared to be statistically true but there was no violation of Art.14, taken with Art.5 in the light of the state's margin of appreciation.

Indirect discrimination

Indirect discrimination may fall within Art.14, but in practice is difficult to prove. The existence of "reasonable and objective justification" for discrimination must be assessed in relation to the "aim and effects" of the measure concerned: *Belgian Linguistic Case (No.2)* (1968).

Draft Protocol 12

In December 2000 the UK refused to sign the draft protocol which would provide an independent right not to be discriminated against by a public authority in respect of "any right set forth by law".

9. REMEDIES FOR VIOLATIONS OF HUMAN RIGHTS

"For all its revolutionary advances," Dinah Shelton has observed, "human rights law has yet to develop a coherent theory or consistent practice of remedies for victims of human rights violations" (*Remedies in International Human Rights Law* (Oxford, 1999)). She attributes this to the sudden development and unprecedented nature of international human rights law, which in Sheldon's view, "displays an uneven proliferation of international complaints mechanisms and techniques that has created a mixture of remedies", ranging from declaratory judgments to awards of widely differing amounts of compensatory damages to orders for specific state action. She quotes a former judge of the European Court of Human Rights stating privately: "We have no principles", to which another judge responds: "We have principles, we just don't apply them.". This Chapter discusses the extent to which incoherence and inconsistency in the award of compensation for breaches of human rights in the European Court of Human Rights will affect the implementation of the Human Rights Act 1998.

Just satisfaction

Article 13 of the European Convention provides:

> "Everyone whose rights and freedoms as set forth in this Convention are violated shall have an effective remedy before a national authority nothwithstanding that the violation has been committed by persons acting in an official capacity".

This Article has not been incorporated into English law by the Human Rights Act, since in the government's view the Act itself gives effect to Art.13 by establishing a scheme under which Convention rights can be raised before our domestic courts and provides an exhaustive code of remedies for those whose Convention rights have been violated so that nothing more is needed.

The Act provides that in relation to any act (or proposed act) of a public authority which the courts find to be unlawful they may grant such relief or remedy, or make such order, within their powers as they consider just and appropriate. This means that the full gamut of remedies available in corresponding domestic law cases, together with most categories of damages and such ancillary remedies as injunctions, are available in human rights cases.

Declaration of incompatibility

Because of the way the Strasbourg jurisprudence has developed however, some forms of damages such as punitive damages are not available in the human rights jurisdiction. An additional, completely new, remedy is the declaration of incompatibility, a means by which the court can state that a particular legislative provision does not comply with human rights standards. Such a declaration can only be made by a competent court and then only if notice has been given to the relevant government department so that it can make representations to the court as to why a declaration should not be made. Competent courts are the High Court, Court of Appeal and House of Lords. The making of a declaration of incompatibility does not absolve the court from applying the legislation concerned, but it does allow the minister, by order, to amend the legislation rapidly with a view to removing the incompatibility. The procedure for making such a remedial order is set out in Sch.2 to the Act and requires that a draft of the order be tabled and approved after at least 60 days by resolution of both Houses of Parliament. There is provision, where the matter is urgent, for the minister to seek parliamentary approval without having tabled a draft in advance. A wide range of options is thus available to a court considering whether to grant relief under the 1998 Human Rights Act. (See p.44).

Discretion

Section 8 of the 1998 Act requires courts to award damages for human rights violations where it is "just and appropriate" and "necessary to afford just satisfaction" to do so. This means that the relief is at the discretion of the court, as it always has been in judicial review proceedings. Where the court finds that an act or proposed act of a public authority is or would be unlawful, it may grant such relief or remedy, or make such order, within its powers, as it considers just and appropriate. Damages can be awarded only by a court which has power to award damages or to order the payment of compensation in civil proceedings. This appears to include both the civil and the criminal divisions of the Court of Appeal. Most tribunals at present have no jurisdiction to award damages, but damages are already available in judicial review proceedings and claimants can thus apply for them under the 1998 Act in judicial review proceedings. The power to award damages under the Human Rights Act has many novel features but it seems to fall short of the creation of a full "constitutional tort". Unlike common law tort damages, damages under the Act are not recoverable as of right. It is submitted that principles such as causation, remoteness and mitigation, which would restrict the scope of damages at common law, are inappropriate where fundamental rights have been breached. The better view, for which Clayton and Tomlinson argue in *The Law of Human Rights*, (OUP, 2000), is that s.8 should be regarded as creating a "public law remedy".

Judicial acts

Damages are specifically excluded under the Act in respect of judicial acts done in good faith, reflecting the existing common law principle. However, there is special provision in s.9(3) for the award of damages against the Crown to compensate victims of judicial acts which breach Art.5(5) of the Convention, covering arrest or detention in breach of the Convention rights to liberty and security. This may override the general exclusion of remedies for good faith judicial acts. Judicial acts are not treated as "unlawful" by the Strasbourg court unless they have involved the court exceeding its jurisdiction.

Alternative remedies

Damages should not be awarded if there is another remedy or exercise of the court's power, which would afford just satisfaction to the person whose rights have been infringed. A public authority which has been held liable in damages can claim contribution from any other person who would be liable in respect of the same damage, for example where a second public authority is involved in the violation.

Victims

A victim for the purposes of the Act includes "any person, non-governmental organisation or group of individuals claiming to be the victim of a violation", and must be able to show that he or she has been directly affected by the alleged violation of the Convention, or is at risk of being affected. The Strasbourg court has tended to allow applications where the applicant is unsure whether the measure complained of will be applied to him. Actions can be brought on behalf of victims by representatives, including a trade union, where the union can show that the members concerned have authorised it to act for them. Though the Strasbourg court could deal only with cases in which all domestic remedies had been exhausted, no such restriction applies to the enforcement of Convention rights in the domestic courts. Section 11 provides that a person's reliance on a Convention right does not restrict any other right or freedom conferred on him in UK law, or his right to enforce such rights.

Other relief

Where the treatment of the claimant would give him claims under the convention and under UK domestic law, he can take up both or either as he chooses. In determining the amount of any award under the Act, the court will take account of any other relief or remedy granted by another court for the same violation. It appears a victim will not be shut out from seeking a remedy under the Act merely because he might be awarded relief in another court.

Level of damages

A notable feature of the Strasbourg case law is the absence of clear principles as to when damages should be awarded and how they should be measured. Part of the reason for this may be that the European Court of Human Rights is not rigidly bound by its previous decisions and has tended to assess each case on its facts, frequently without considering or distinguishing similar cases. A similar approach to assessment of damages is adopted by the French domestic courts. The ECHR is a large court with judges from many different backgrounds, who may have varying experiences of awarding damages. The level of damages awarded in Strasbourg has been relatively low, partly because the court has been anxious not to offend member governments and their populations in controversial cases.

The absence of clear principles for awarding and setting damages gives rise to a problem for the UK courts in applying the

Human Rights Act, given that they are bound by statute to have regard to the principles established in Strasbourg. What is clear is that damages are awarded by the European Court of Human Rights only where the court has found a violation, the domestic law of the respondent state allows only "partial reparation" and the award is necessary to afford just satisfaction. The general aim of awarding damages in the Strasbourg court is to compensate the victim for the losses suffered as a result of the breach of his rights, and to return him as far as possible to the position he would have occupied if the breach had not occurred. In some cases, however, the nature of the breach precludes complete reparation, and the claimant will be limited to just satisfaction (see, *e.g. Konig v Germany* (1980) and *Smith and Grady v UK* (1998)).

Heads of damages

The Strasbourg court has often awarded a global sum without breaking it down into different heads of damages. But on occasion it has broke down awards under three heads: pecuniary loss, non-pecuniary loss and costs and expenses. The first category can include loss of earnings, loss of pension rights, medical expenses and unlawfully expropriated property. Non-pecuniary loss has included compensation for pain and suffering, distress, inconvenience and loss of reputation. "Loss of relationship", as a result, for example, of wrongful imprisonment, may also qualify for compensation. Companies as well as individuals can be awarded compensation for non-pecuniary loss (*Comingersoll SA v Portugal* (2000)). Reasonable costs and expenses are awarded only where they were actually and necessarily incurred to prevent or obtain redress, and can include costs incurred in the domestic courts on the way to the European Court of Human Rights. It seems likely in any event that the UK courts will apply normal domestic rules to determine costs.

State remedies

In assessing what constitutes just satisfaction the court will take into account measures taken by the respondent state. A retrial may be sufficient redress for a violation of the right to a fair trial, for example. In some cases remission of sentence or a pardon may remove the need for any further award, but in *Ringeisen v Austria* (1972), the court held that deduction of time spent in detention on remand from a prison sentence could not constitute full restitution because no freedom was given to replace the freedom unlawfully taken away. Even where a full pardon had been granted, there was still room for compensation for loss of opportunities: *Bönisch v Austria* (1986). Where the case has resulted in a change in the law, this may be treated as adequate just satisfaction without the need for financial compensation: *Dudgeon v UK* (1983).

No award

Quite frequently, the court's finding of a violation has been held to constitute sufficient satisfaction, since the mere fact of violation in itself is not considered to justify an award: *Golder v UK* (1975). However, the practice is not wholly consistent. The court is more likely to hold that a judgment provides just satisfaction where the breach in question is procedural. Judgment does not seem to be considered as sufficient satisfaction for pecuniary loss. Small non-pecuniary losses may be ignored.

Seriousness of breach

In assessing whether to award damages, and if so how much, the court will take into account the seriousness of the violation of the victim's human rights. The full damages claim was awarded in respect of a Turkish claimant who had been tortured as a suspected terrorist but eventually released without charge: *Aksoy v Turkey* (1998). These are not expressly stated to be aggravated damages, and claims for aggravated damages have been dismissed. Claims for punitive damages have generally been unsuccessful, apparently because they are not compatible with the aim of full restitution. Offensive conduct by the state has in the past attracted increased damages, and the court may also take account of the state's record of previous violations. The claimant's conduct is another factor to be taken into account in arriving at compensation. Damages are less often awarded to claimants who are criminals.

Causal link

One rule which is strictly applied is that there must be a clear causal link between the violation and the loss. For example, applicants who had to wait an unreasonable amount of time to be tried and imprisoned for fraud were not compensated for the losses resulting from the collapse of their business and their inability to engage in professional activities, since they resulted from the prosecution itself and not from the delay. Where the breach resulted from a judge's having taken decisions on the case despite having been involved at an earlier stage as investigating magistrate, the court refused to speculate what might have happened had the proceedings been conducted fairly. However, in a case where the claimant had been driven into bankruptcy by delay in proceedings to recover money owed to him, the court took the view that there had been a loss of opportunities which ought to be compensated in damages: *Moreira de Azeveda v Portugal* (1990). In *Bönisch v Austria* (1986), damages for loss of opportunities were awarded even though the prospects of realising them were questionable, apparently despite the absence of a clear causal link. Similarly, in *H v UK* (1988), the claimant's loss of relationship with her daughter might have occurred even if proceedings had been conducted expeditiously, but the court refused to exclude the possibility that speedier proceedings might have had a different outcome, and did award damages for loss of opportunity.

Speculative losses

There is thus an area of uncertainty, but the court has declined to clarify its position on speculative losses. In some cases based on violations of the claimant's procedural rights, the court itself has been willing to assess what the outcome of correctly conducted proceedings would have been. The Law Commission, which reviewed the cases in this area, concluded that the court's decisions were impossible to reconcile, adding:

> "One can only guess that in some cases the Court feels sympathy towards certain applicants based on the particular circumstances and will go out of its way to award damages despite the usual requirement of a clear causal link".

Full restitution

Interest is treated as an element of full restitution, though the basis on which it may be awarded is less clear. Awards appear to have been confined largely to pecuniary claims. The Law Commission considered the possible application of the principle of full restitution under s.8 of the 1998 Act and concluded that the

English courts were not bound in every case to follow Strasbourg precedents and would determine the majority of cases according to the normal common law rules for determining damages. The government has explained the provisions of s.8 on the basis that it is aimed at ensuring people receive in the domestic courts damages equivalent to what they would have obtained had they gone to Strasbourg. This may mean that as a general rule the domestic courts would not normally award damages of a kind not available in Strasbourg, nor deny damages for a loss which would be compensated by the ECHR, but s.8(4) refers only to the principles applied by the Strasbourg court, which is taken to refer to the basic objectives of the system, rather than their application in individual assessments of damages. The distinction has been considered by the Court of Appeal in *Heil v Rankin* (2000), where Lord Woolf M.R. viewed the court's task as "limited to providing fresh guidelines so as to give effect to well established principles as to the objective which should be achieved by an award of damages". Full compensation was the main objective, applying to non-pecuniary as well as to pecuniary loss. The use which the claimant would make of the money was irrelevant. The extent of pecuniary loss tended to be established by ever more sophisticated calculations, while the scale of damages for non-pecuniary loss remained a jury question.

Contrast with tort damages

The analogy with tort damages is obvious, but could be misleading, because tort damages frequently include a punitive element entirely lacking in the European Human Rights jurisdiction, and because the law of tort does not normally allow recovery for pure economic loss, whereas such recovery is consistent with the objective of full restitution and has been awarded by the Strasbourg court. Loss of relationship is a head of damages compensated in Strasbourg but without an equivalent in UK law. Various technical rules on remoteness are also inconsistent with the thorough application of the Strasbourg principle. In a recent paper, Lord Woolf expressed the view that unlike tort damages, which were payable as of right, damages under the act were discretionary, since the court was enjoined to do what was "just and appropriate" and give "just satisfaction". The absence of Strasbourg principles as to damages, in Woolf's view, would allow the English courts to develop their own principles within the statutory framework. Account should be taken of the fact that damages would be paid out of public funds, not out of a bottomless purse. He said: "an award of damages against a Health Authority can reduce the resources available for treating patients. An award against a Housing Authority can reduce the funds available for providing or repairing homes. There can be numerous victims of the same unlawful act". In his view, account should be taken both of the interests of the complainant and those of society as a whole.

Damages as a last resort

Lord Woolf suggested that damages should only be awarded as a last resort where other remedies would not afford just satisfaction; exemplary or aggravated damages should not be awarded; damages should be moderate, on the low side compared with tort awards, and limited to what is necessary to achieve just satisfaction; damages should compensate the victim for what has happened only "so far as the unlawful conduct exceeds what could lawfully happen"; the victim would be under a duty to mitigate loss; no distinction should be made between pecuniary and non-pecuniary loss and domestic rules as to costs should be followed.

There appear to be limits on the extent to which the English courts can restrict the extent of recovery available under the Act. It is to be noted that the basic requirement is just satisfaction to "the person in whose favour [the order for damages] is made", which apparently precludes the court from taking account, for example, of the possibility that other claimants may also have been affected by the same wrongful act of the state. A claimant who has a quantifiable financial loss appears to be entitled to restitution, provided he meets the other necessary criteria. However, wider policy issues may have some impact on the level of awards for non-pecuniary loss.

These considerations will also no doubt impact on the state, since the state may have the possibility of providing just satisfaction by some non-financial means such as the grant of a pardon coupled with an acknowledgement that the claimant's rights were infringed. However, whereas the Strasbourg court has frequently taken the view that a victim is sufficiently compensated by a finding that his rights have been violated, it is more difficult to see that a ruling by an English court, itself an emanation of the state responsible for the violation, could provide sufficient compensation merely by deciding that there had been a violation of the statute.

In his paper, Lord Woolf suggested that the English courts might consider adopting the criteria used by the European Court of Justice in determining damages for breach of community law by a Member State. The ECJ awards such damages only where there has been a sufficiently serious breach of a rule of law which was intended to confer rights on individuals, and there is a direct causal link between the breach and the damage sustained by the claimant.

Causation and remoteness

The Strasbourg Court does not distinguish between causation and remoteness in the same way as domestic courts. There is no express reference to concepts such as reasonable foreseeability; the requirement of a causal link provides the only express limit to the availability of compensatory damages. In this respect, the Strasbourg practice seems more akin to the domestic approach to intentional torts than non-intentional torts.

Human Rights Act and Damages

The proper approach to damages under the Human Rights Act has been clarified by a strong court of appeal in the *Anufrieja v Southwark LBC* [2003] EWCA Civ 1406. It was claimed that defendants had failed to take positive action to ensure respect for the claimants' rights under Art.8. The court said such positive obligations were not absolute and a claim would arise only where there was an element of culpability in the failure to act. Isolated acts of even significant carelessness were unlikely to suffice. Unlike tort damages, damages for breach of the Convention were not recoverable as of right. Their purpose was to afford "just satisfaction" to an injured party. The court's concern in Convention cases was usually to order an end to the breach of the claimant's rights, and compensation was at most of secondary importance. Damages were only available where the unlawful act of a public authority belonged to a class identified by s.6(1) of the Human Rights Act, and did not include cases where as a result of primary registration the authority could not have acted differently, or where it was putting into effect legislation which was incompatible with a convention right. The court had discretion whether to make an award, which must be necessary to achieve just satisfaction. Exemplary damages were not available.

The court endorsed the discretionary approach to damages taken in two other recent cases, *R. (KB) v Mental Health Review Tribunal* [2003] EWHC 193 (Admin) and *Berbard v Enfield LBC* [2002] EWHC 2282 Admin. Where damages were considered appropriate, it was right to determine the amount by considering comparable claims in tort, or in the case of maladministration, the size of comparable awards by the Ombudsman. A breach of a positive obligation under Art.8 to provide support for family life would really be found, and comparisons would be difficult. Damages should be modest since the cost of supporting those in need fell on society as a whole and resources were limited. Similar considerations would apply in asylum cases, when it was important not to create the impression that asylum seekers were profiting from their status.

The Appeals Court was particularly anxious that the costs of proceedings be kept in proportion. It found that the combined costs were many times greater than damages that could reasonably had been anticipated, and the costs at first instance of each party were totally disproportionate to the amount involved. The courts should look critically at any attempt to recover damages under the Human Rights Act for maladministration by any procedure other than judicial review in the administrative court. The claimant should be required at the application stage to establish that judicial review was more appropriate than complaint to the Parliamentary Commissioner for administration or the Local Government Ombudsman. Where appropriate permission to seek judicial review should be granted on the basis that damages be determined by alternative dispute resolution. The court should not be deluged with extensive written and oral arguments.

Damages under specific Articles

Damages under s.8(3) should not be nominal, since the purpose is to achieve "just satisfaction", nor for the same reason should they be exemplary or punitive.

Article 2 claims are rare. The ECtHR refused to award damages of any sort in *McCann v UK* (1996), because the victims had been intending to plant a bomb, though costs were awarded to the complainants. Awards of damages for breach of Art.2 have been made against Turkey in a number of cases arising from the conflict in Kurdistan (*Kaya v Turkey* (1998); *Güleç v Turkey* (1998)).

Article 3

The Strasbourg court has refused to order damages in cases concerning threatened rather than actual breaches of Art.3, the prohibition on torture. In *Soering v UK* (1989), where the claimant successfully resisted extradition to the United States on a capital charge, the court declared that its finding amounted to just satisfaction, though the claimant was awarded costs. There was a similar finding in *Chahal v UK* (1997), concerning the threat to deport a Sikh leader to India, where he might have been tortured. By contrast, actual torture in breach of Art.3 has been compensated with substantial damages awards. These include £25,000 for a victim of rape and torture at the hands of security forces (*Aydin v Turkey* (1997)) and £6,500 for a victim of assault by police officers (*Ribitsch v Austria* (1995)). Failure by the authorities to investigate allegations of torture (*e.g.* by police) can result in the award of damages.

Effect of Article 5(5)

Article 5(5) provides: "Everyone who has been the victim of arrest or detention in contravention of the provisions of this Article shall have an enforceable right to compensation". An order is not "unlawful" in this context merely because it is overturned for error of law or even on *Wednesbury* grounds (*Associated Provincial Picture Houses Ltd v Wednesbury Corporation* (1948)). The court must have gone beyond its "jurisdiction". The difficulty is in defining the limits of that term in English administrative law, in which, for most purposes, the differences between jurisdictional and non-jurisdictional errors have disappeared.

A period of detention will in principle be lawful if it is carried out pursuant to a court order. A subsequent finding that the court erred under domestic law in making the order will not necessarily retrospectively affect the validity of the intervening period of detention. For this reason, the Strasbourg organs have consistently refused to uphold applications from persons convicted of criminal offences who complain that their convictions or sentences were found by the appellate courts to have been based on errors of fact or law (*Benham v UK* (1996)). The principles of English law which should be taken into account in this case distinguished between acts of a magistrates' court which were within its jurisdiction and those which were in excess of jurisdiction. The former were valid and effective unless or until they were overturned by a superior court, whereas the latter were null and void from the outset.

(1) The question whether the detention is "lawful" is to be determined in accordance with national law, and, in the first instance, by the national courts.

(2) Detention pursuant to a court order may be "lawful", even if it is subsequently found on appeal that the court erred in fact or law. The issue of "lawfulness" under Article 5 is one of jurisdiction.

(3) In the context of English law (apparently, following agreement between the parties), this issue was treated as equivalent to the issue of jurisdiction raised by the pre-1990 law on justices' immunity.

(4) The court felt able to distinguish *R. v Manchester City Magistrates' Court, Ex p. Davies* (1989), on the basis that there the magistrates had "failed altogether" to carry out the inquiry required by law, whereas in the present case the magistrates had addressed that question but had reached a finding which could not be sustained on the evidence.

(5) The court did not purport itself to rule on the position under English law, but reached its conclusion on the basis that it had not been established "with any degree of certainty" that the English court had found an excess of jurisdiction under English law.

Remedies in judicial review proceedings

The traditional remedies available on judicial review are mandamus (now mandatory order), certiorari (quashing order), prohibition (prohibiting order), injunction, declaration, and damages. The first three remedies, known as prerogative orders, are available only on judicial review. Declarations and injunctions have the same effect in judicial review as in private law actions, but the discretion to make them is broader in the public law context. Damages cannot be awarded unless the court is satisfied that such damages could have been awarded if the claimant had brought private law proceedings to recover them.

Interim relief is also available by way of injunction. Clayton and Tomlinson highlight the issue of whether an interim injunction should be granted to restrain a public authority from acting incompatibly with Convention rights pending the substantive hearing. This is likely to be decided on the balance of convenience (*American Cyanamid v Ethicon* (1975)), but such an injunction will not be available when the public authority is acting in accordance with statutory rights, since the court cannot disapply primary legislation.

Since judicial review remedies are discretionary, they may be refused where alternative remedies or rights of appeal are available to the claimant. They can also be refused if it is felt that the claimant's conduct is a bar to relief. Delay (including a failure to bring proceedings promptly even where they are brought within the statutory time limit) may preclude a remedy. And the court may take the view that likely effects of granting the remedy are such that it should not be done.

Remedies in criminal proceedings

Where a defendant in criminal proceedings establishes that his Convention rights have been violated, he has a variety of potential remedies, depending on the nature and circumstances of the breach. These include an order that the summons be withdrawn, the quashing of an indictment, a stay of the proceedings, an order excluding evidence or requiring the inclusion of evidence, an order of the Court of Appeal (or the Divisional Court in proceedings by way of case stated) quashing a conviction.

Human rights points should be raised in the criminal proceedings themselves, not in parallel judicial review proceedings (*R. v Secretary of State for the Home Department, Ex p. Kebilene* (1999)). A stay of proceedings could be sought in cases where a charge is incompatible with Convention rights, for example, because it infringes freedom of expression or assembly; where a prosecution is deliberately brought in breach of Convention rights, a position similar to common law abuse of process. Where the prosecution involves a breach of rights other than those under Art.6 a stay is likely to be granted only if the defendant can establish prejudice, and where rights to a fair trial have been infringed, a stay is likely only where it can be shown that a fair trial is no longer possible.

Exclusion of evidence

The existing test for the exclusion of evidence, based on s.78 of PACE, was conserved in *Nottingham City Council v Amin* (2000), where Lord Bingham C.J. held that the proper test was whether or not admission would deny the defendant a fair trial. This "fairness" is criticised as inadequate by Clayton and Tomlinson, who argue on the basis of European and Commonwealth authorities that the rationale for excluding evidence through a breach of a convention right ought to be: (i) the vindication of the right, denying the prosecution the possibility of profiting from the breach of the convention; (ii) the preservation of the integrity of the judicial system. However, this is contrary to the existing common law trend, and it is more likely that the exclusionary power will be exercised narrowly.

In *R. v Looseley* (see also p.91) the House of Lords reviewed the situations where a finding of entrapment might lead either to a stay of prosecution, the exclusion of evidence or mitigation of sentence. It refined the test set out in earlier cases such as *Amin*. If the law enforcement officer does not have reasonable grounds for suspicion or even if he does have reasonable grounds goes further than providing an "unexceptional opportunity" then the conduct was entrapment. The predisposition of the defendant was not relevant. A key consideration was maintaining the integrity of the criminal justice system. The decision while leaving the law uncertain indicates a shift towards the jurisprudential approach advocated by Clayton and Tomlinson.

---

10. THE EUROPEAN UNION AND HUMAN RIGHTS

The European Union has frequently proclaimed and emphasised its commitment to human rights. The Amsterdam Treaty states: "The Union is founded on the principles of liberty, democracy, respect for human rights and the rule of law", adding specifically that the Union will respect the European Human Rights Convention. States which engage in serious and persistent violations of human rights can lose their rights under the EU treaty (in effect, be expelled). However, there has been a perceived lack of a comprehensive or coherent policy for implementing human rights within the EU. Some experts have expressed strong doubts as to whether the Union's institutions possess adequate legal competence in relation to a wide range of issues arising within the framework of EU policies. Some of the problems were highlighted by *Matthews v UK* (1999), decided by the European Court of Human Rights. The applicant was a Gibraltar resident denied the opportunity of voting in elections for the European Parliament because of the limited scope of the European Community's direct election provisions. She claimed that the direct election provisions infringed her right of free election under Art.3, Protocol 1 to the European Convention on Human Rights. The court found in her favour, paving the way for intervention by the European Court of Human Rights into areas which had been thought to be purely a matter for the European Court of Justice.

GENERAL PRINCIPLES

The EU is not a state and has not itself signed the Convention. However, the European Court of Justice, responsible for ensuring observance of EU law, has said that the general principles of EU law enshrine fundamental human rights, and has recognised the Convention as having special significance as a source of EU Law principles.

The general principles of EU law are implicit rather than explicit and derive from Arts 220, 230 and 288 of the EU treaty: Art.220 states: "The Court of Justice shall ensure that in the implementation and application of this treaty the law is observed". Article 230 sets out the powers and jurisdiction of the court to review the legality of acts of the EU Council and Commission on various grounds, including the infringement of "any rule of law", while Art.288 refers to "the general principles common to the laws of the member states".

The main principles are:

Fundamental rights

The expectation of the founders of the European Community was that citizens' rights, and their protection against unlawful interference by the Community, would be sufficiently safeguarded by national law. However, this expectation was over-optimistic.

Proportionality

This requires the court to balance the interests of the individual with that of the wider public interest. The degree of scrutiny of the administrative action by the European Court of Justice depends on the context. Thus an individual right unduly restricted by administrative action will be strictly enforced. An excessive administrative penalty will be enforced, but not as strictly. And where the policy objective is itself disproportionate the administrative action will be subject only to limited scrutiny.

Equality

Persons in similar situations should not be treated differently unless such treatment is objectively justified.

Legal certainty

Legal certainty is concerned with achieving a fair balance between the EU's own need to alter its policies for the future, and the needs of individuals to base their activities on pre-existing norms. It has two aspects. The first, legitimate expectation, can be invoked by a litigant in the European Court of Justice as a rule of interpretation, as a basis for an action for damages in tort and the basis for annulment of an EU measure. The second aspect, non-retroactivity, is a presumption that EU legislation is not retro-active. This presumption can be rebutted by clear contrary evidence, provided the legitimate expectations of those concerned are respected.

Procedural rights

These include the right to a hearing, the right to due process and the duty to give reasons.

Subsidiarity

The Community can take action only insofar as the Member States cannot sufficiently achieve the objectives of the proposed action, so that because of the scale or effects of the proposed action, it can be better achieved by the Community.

Solidarity

Member States must take all appropriate measures to comply with their obligations under EU law.

Specific Convention rights

Among the individual Convention rights explicitly recognised by the European Court of Justice are:

(a) The right to own property (Protocol, Art.1);
(b) Non-retroactivity of penal provisions (Art.7);
(c) Right to privacy (Art.8);
(d) Freedom of religion (Art.9).

By the Amsterdam treaty, the EU member states agreed that: "The EU shall respect fundamental rights, as guaranteed by the European Convention on Human Rights and as they result from the constitutional traditions common to the member states, as general principles of Community law".

Wadham and Mountfield pointed out that in some instances it may be better to challenge incompatible primary legislation through EU law rather than through the Human Rights Act 1998 (*Blackstone's Guide to the Human Rights Act* (1998, 2000)). If primary legislation is found to contravene directly effective EU legislation the national court is bound to disapply the primary legislation. By contrast, under the Human Rights Act the court can only be asked to make a declaration of incompatibility. In addition, EU procedure allows more scope for representative action by such groups as trade unions or pressure groups.

EU CHARTER OF FUNDAMENTAL RIGHTS

In the face of pressure for a more coherent human rights approach, the heads of state and government decided at the Cologne summit on June 4, 1999 that an EU Charter of Fundamental Rights would be drawn up, including general rights of liberty and equality as well as economic and social rights. A Convention made up of 15 representatives of heads of state or government, 16 Euro-MPs, 30 members of national parliaments and a representative of the President of the European Commission has since produced a draft Charter. The Charter was proclaimed at the Nice Conference in December 2000 but was not made part of the subsequent Treaty.

Reasons why a human rights policy is needed for the EU, include the movement towards a closer Union with a comprehensive single market; the increase in racism, xenophobia and ethnic hatred in Europe; the tendency towards a "Fortress Europe", hostile to outsiders and discouraging to refugees and asylum-seekers; the need for adequate safeguards for human rights where there is international co-operation on policy and security matters; the extensive powers of the EU bureaucracy and the planned expansion of the EU.

The Draft Charter has been criticised, for example by the Law Society, because it is aimed only at EU citizens and does not, unlike the European Convention on Human Rights, protect others under the jurisdiction of EU Member States. It is divided into "chapters" (see below). It is expected eventually to become legally binding but is currently a matter of controversy. Its preamble states:

> "In adopting this Charter the Union intends to enhance the protection of fundamental rights in the light of changes in society, social progress and scientific and technological developments by making those rights more visible".

The sources of the rights in the Charter include the constitutional traditions common to the Member States, the EU Treaty and the Community Treaties, the European Convention on Human Rights, the Social Charters adopted by the Community and by the Council of Europe and the case law of the Court of Justice of the European Communities and of the European Court of Human Rights. The draft Charter states: "Enjoyment of these rights entails responsibilities and duties with regard to other persons, to the human community and to future generations". The draft Charter also states "The charter should ... include the fundamental rights that pertain only to the Union's citizens", the clear implication being that no additional "rights" are to be granted to migrants, refugees or asylum-seekers. The main outcome will be a Convention to enforce these rights. The process of determining what is to be included in the Charter and the Convention is to stay firmly in the hands of the Council. A consultative "body" will be set up comprised of representatives of member states, the European and national parliaments and the Commission. The European Court of Justice will have an "advisory" role while "representatives of social groups and experts should be invited to give their views".

In 2003 the draft EU Constitution was published. This seeks to incorporate the EU Charter on Fundamental Rights into the EU Treaties. This is a controversial matter since the Charter, unlike the Convention, protects economic and social rights. Under the Constitution the Charter would be legally enforceable. In addition the Constitution provides that the European Union should itself accede to the ECHR. The Chapter of the Charter are:

Dignity

Chapter 1 is headed "Dignity" and asserts in its first Article that human dignity is inviolable and must be respected and protected. Article 2 enshrines the right to life and prohibits death sentences and execution. Article 3 sets out a right to integrity of the person, including a requirement that free and informed consent be secured for medical intervention and prohibiting eugenic practices, human cloning and the making of money from the sale of human body parts. Prohibitions on torture and slavery mirror those in the European Convention on Human Rights.

Freedoms

Under Chapter 2, "Freedoms", Art.6 simply asserts the rights to liberty and security of person and respect for private and family life, while setting out detailed provisions on the protection of personal data, which "must be processed fairly for specified purposes and on the basis of the consent of the person concerned or some other legitimate basis laid down by law". It provides for individuals to have a right of access to data which has been collected about them, the right to have it rectified and compliance to be under the control of an independent authority.

Other rights in this chapter are the right to marry and found a family, the right to freedom of thought, conscience and religion, including the right to conscientious objection, freedom of expression and information; freedom of assembly and of association; freedom of the arts and sciences and respect for academic freedom; a right to education and to have access to vocational and continuing training, including a right to receive free compulsory education and a freedom to found educational establishments. There is provision for freedom to choose an occupation, conduct a business and own property, including intellectual property. Finally there, is a right to asylum in accordance with the relevant international agreements, and a prohibition on collective expulsions and the removal of anyone to a state which might put them to death or torture them.

Equality

Chapter 3, "Equality", provides for equality before the law, prohibiting discrimination on any ground such as sex, race, colour, ethnic or social origin, genetic features, language, religion or belief, political or any other opinion, membership of a national minority, property, birth, disability, age or sexual orientation. It guarantees respect for cultural, religious and linguistic diversity, equality between men and women, the rights of the child and the integration of persons with disabilities.

Solidarity

Chapter 4, "Solidarity", enshrines workers' right to information and consultation within the undertaking, to negotiate and conclude collective agreements and to take collective action to defend their interests, including strike action, "in accordance with Community law and national laws and practices". Everyone is to have a right of access to a free placement service, a right to protection against unjustified dismissal and to enjoy fair and just working conditions. Child labour is prohibited and young people admitted to work must have appropriate working conditions. The family is to enjoy legal, economic and social protection with a right to protection from dismissal for a reason connected with maternity and the right to paid maternity leave and to parental leave following the birth or adoption of a child. There are also guarantees of social security and social assistance, health care, and environmental and consumer protection

Citizens' rights

Chapter 5, Citizens' rights, includes the right to vote and stand as a candidate, a right to good administration, a right of access to documents, an EU Ombudsman, a right to petition the European Parliament and rights to freedom of movement and of residence and diplomatic and consular protection.

Justice General Provisions

Chapter 6 covers rights in the sphere of justice, and Chapter 7 contains general provisions about the scope of the rights embodied in the draft Charter.

11. SAMPLE QUESTIONS AND MODEL ANSWERS

Note: In the vast majority of instances where human rights issues are raised this will be alongside pre-existing areas of law, whether it is criminal law, the law of tort, administrative law or the law of evidence, for example. The answers to the questions below, however, have exclusively concentrated on the matters relevant to the application of the Human Rights Act in order to identify the specific changes it has brought about. Students here are not therefore required to demonstrate knowledge of the other areas of substantive law, although this would not of course be the position in practice.

QUESTION 1

The scheme of the Human Rights Act upholds existing constitutional principles. The Act is therefore leading to evolutionary rather than revolutionary change.
  Discuss.

Answer

The three main constitutional principles referred to in the question are the sovereignty of Parliament, the separation of powers and the rule of law. The sovereignty of parliament is the principle that the courts will enforce Acts which have been approved by Parliament and have received Royal Assent. This has been the central principle of the Constitution, at least since the so-called Glorious Revolution of 1689. When Parliament invited William and Mary to take the throne previously occupied by James II, it imposed a set of conditions in the form of a Bill of Rights. The central principle of that Bill is the sovereignty of Parliament and the rights with which the Bill is concerned are those of Parliament rather than what we would now regard as "human rights". Separation of powers refers to the division between executive, legislative and judicial branches of government. In the UK this principle is far from absolute, the Lord Chancellor, whose responsibilities are now limited in the Constitutional Reform Bill 2004, has had a prominent role in all three branches of government. In practice the principle consists largely of the principle of the independence of the judiciary from the executive. This is closely tied to the third principle, that of the rule of law. This embodies the idea that the executive must act within the law and subject its decisions to the jurisdiction of the judiciary.

The development of the British constitution since 1688 has been piecemeal the principle, but the principle central to the Bill of Rights has not changed. In other countries such as France, the United States, Germany and South Africa, constitutional change resulted from revolution or some other great social upheaval, such as military defeat. The Human Rights Act, by contrast, did not emerge from a social upheaval but is part of a political programme of constitutional reform which has other facets such as devolution and the development of new forms of urban local government. This essay examines the extent to which the constitutional principles referred to above are accommodated in the scheme of the Act. It also looks at the changes that have arisen from the enforcement of the Act.

The draftsmen of the Human Rights Act have been careful to ensure that, at least from the formal standpoint, it does not infringe parliamentary sovereignty. The courts continue to enforce Acts of Parliament whether or not they accord with the European Convention on Human Rights. They will, however, read and give effect to both primary and secondary legislation "in a way which is compatible with Convention rights". Any ambiguity in a provision should be resolved in favour of that interpretation which is compatible with the Convention. Account must be taken of the judgments of the ECtHR and the decisions of the now defunct Commission. This does not undermine parliamentary sovereignty because it means that Parliament has itself resolved that in future its Acts must be interpreted to accord with the Convention, but it does give a greater role to judicial creativity in the interpretation of legislation which impinges on Convention rights.

The Act also introduces a change in parliamentary procedure, the "statement of compatibility". This obliges the relevant minister prior to the second reading of a Bill in either House to make a written statement, either that the measure is compatible with the Convention or that it is not possible to make such a statement but the government nonetheless wishes to press ahead with it. The fact that the minister has made a statement of compatibility does not in any way oblige a court to find that the Act is compatible with the Convention. However, it does mean that ministers will have to put their minds to the effect of proposed legislation on Convention rights and to give notice if they plan to do away with any of the rights embodied in the Convention. Were that to happen consistency would probably demand that the government derogate from the relevant Article or Articles of the Convention, or in the extreme case denounce the Convention as a whole.

The contrast is striking between the way in which the Convention has been incorporated and the approach adopted to European law when Britain joined the European Community. Here Parliament ceded to the European institutions part of its power to determine the law, or (on another view) decided that until further notice English courts would enforce the decisions of the Council of Ministers and the European Court of Justice. Nothing of the sort has been attempted in the human rights field. Even the manner in which the Convention has been incorporated, Article by Article rather than as a whole, and with certain Articles (such as Art.13) omitted, is resolutely piecemeal and cautious. The path to incorporation has also been smoothed by an extensive and expensive programme of judicial education. There has been no question of shoving the whole package onto a resistant judiciary.

Instead of giving courts the power to strike down Acts of Parliament in the name of human rights, as Acts of Congress can be struck down if found unconstitutional by the Supreme Court in the United States, the most a court can do under the Act is to make a declaration of incompatibility, drawing attention to the contradiction between the legislative provision and Convention rights and leaving Parliament to decide whether or not to remove the incompatibility. Such a declaration can be made only by a superior court and only after the minister concerned has had an opportunity of being represented and making submissions in relation to the declaration.

The impact on the separation of powers is mixed. The requirement that the judiciary be independent has already had an impact, upsetting the Scottish sheriff court system, which relied on the appointment of untenured deputies from among senior lawyers (see *Storrs and Chalmers* (2000)). These were not independent of the Scottish law officers because their subsequent progress depended on executive favour. The position of the Lord Chancellor might also come under challenge, since his is a political appointment made by the Prime Minister and as a Cabinet Minister he cannot be regarded as independent, particularly where the government is a party to the litigation. At the same time, however, the role of the judiciary will become more political, as judges will characteristically be asked to decide whether restrictions on rights are necessary in a democratic society and whether the actions of government in the widest sense are proportional. These are at bottom political decisions.

The extent of the observance of constitutional principles has led to much academic debate as to how far the judiciary have been overcautious or excessively robust. There are indications that the government perceives some judicial decisions as encroaching too much on the role of the executive. This is seen for example in the Home Secretary's reaction to the decision of Collins J. on asylum seekers. The case was about the Home Secretary's duty to support asylum seekers and the court decided that the Home Office were in breach of Art.6 in refusing the applicants the right to have their individual circumstances examined and to appeal if denied benefits. David Blunkett complained about a situation where parliament debates issues and the judges overturn them.

Other examples of a robust judicial approach are the House of Lords decisions in *Daly* (2001) which gave content to the key principle of proportionality in judicial review, and *R. (Razgar) v Secretary of State for the Home Department* (2004) which held that Art.8 could be engaged by the foreseeable consequences for health of removal from the United Kingdom pursuant to an immigration decision. The courts have also used their powers to interpret legislation in the light of Convention principles in a way which some have argued has flouted the will of parliament. An example is *R. v A* (2001) where the view of the minority was that the majority House of Lords decision turned the will of parliament on its head.

On balance, however, the courts have taken the stance that in respecting constitutional niceties it is preferable to be cautious. This approach is seen in four areas. First of all, policy considerations have been weighed against Convention rights. Thus in *Brown v Stott* (2001) the Privy Council held that the public interest in enforcing drink-driving legislation had to be balanced against the right to a fair trial. Secondly, the approach to the retrospective effect of the Human Rights Act has been minimalist, as seen for example in *R. v Kansal* (2001), criticised by the Strasbourg Court in *Kansal v UK* (2004). Thirdly, a restrictive approach has been taken to the scope of the definition of public authority under the Act, as for example in *Aston Cantlow Parochial Church Council v Wallbank* (2003).

Above all, however, the judiciary have shown reluctance to issue declarations of incompatibility. Thus in *Wilson v First County Trust Ltd (No.2)* (2001) the House of Lords took the view both that it had jurisdiction to make a declaration of incompatibility concerning events that predated the enforcement of the Human Rights Act and also that the concept of proportionality should be restrictively applied. Lord Nicholls stressed that the courts had a "revising role". He stated, "Parliament is charged with the primary responsibility for deciding whether the means chosen to deal with a social problem are both necessary and appropriate." In one case where a declaration was issued, *International Transport Roth GmbH v Secretary of State for the Home Department* (2002), the powerful dissenting judgment of Laws L.J. expressed the need to observe constitutional principles. He drew attention to the differing roles which fell properly to the courts or to parliament and the executive. He referred to the two latter as the "democratic powers". This approach emphasises that it is for the legislature and the executive to effect substantive changes to the law rather than judicial creativity. As Lord Hoffmann observed in *Alconbury* "the Human Rights Act 1998 was no doubt intended to strengthen the rule of law but not to inaugurate the rule of lawyers." Evolution not revolution seems to predominate.

QUESTION 2

"Whilst our domestic courts appear to be unwilling to recognise a free-standing privacy right actionable under Article 8 such a right continues to flourish in Strasbourg . . . " (*Rosalind English and Philip Havers* (2003) 6 EHRLR 587–600)

Discuss.

Answer

Until the coming into force of the Human Rights Act 1998 it was a commonplace that breach of privacy was not a cause of action in English law. Somebody whose privacy was breached might have a remedy in the related area of breach of confidence, where equity had developed a body of authority on the foundations laid in *Prince Albert v Strange* (1849). But although in the absence of a specific privacy tort the courts interpreted confidence widely, an action was only open where privacy had been breached by a breach of confidence. The draftsmen of Art.8 of the European Convention probably had in the forefront of their minds the need to proscribe state interference with citizens' private life, and it is only gradually that the right to respect for private and family life, home and correspondence has come to be seen as a potential right enforceable against the world.

Privacy stands at an intersection of competing interests, powerful media interests favour openness in the guise of freedom of speech, while on the other hand celebrities, politicians, film and pop stars, sportsmen and the like, have an interest in limiting or controlling access to the details of their lives. One of the paradoxes of this area is that those whose celebrity is based on publicising themselves are among the most vocal advocates of privacy rights. Media interests would say that such people ought not to enjoy the benefits of publicity without having to bear its burdens. If celebrities could control their publicity completely it would be little more than free advertising, say the media.

The most often quoted expression of judicial enthusiasm for a free-standing privacy right was an *obiter dictum* of Lord Justice Sedley in interlocutory proceedings in *Douglas v Hello* (2000), a case which was eventually decided on the basis of breach of confidence, rather than of privacy. Sedley said: "The law no longer needs to construct an artificial relationship of confidentiality between intruder and victim: it can recognise privacy itself as a legal principle drawn from the fundamental value of personal autonomy" As subsequent cases have shown, however, this view is not universally shared among the judiciary, with many judges reluctant to innovate in an area where parliament has itself been loath to intervene. When the *Douglas* case came to be decided on its merits, Lindsay J. upheld their breach of confidence action, but firmly dismissed their privacy claim. He doubted the existence of a free-standing privacy right and considered that even if such a right were required, it would have await a case which could not be dealt with any other way.

The issue has not gone away, however, and has cropped up in various contexts since. In *Jones v University of Warwick* (2003), the Court of Appeal held that covert filming of a personal injury claimant by an inquiry agent did not breach privacy rights. And in *Maddock v Devon County Council* (2003), there was no privacy breach where information in the claimant's social service files was disclosed to a university where she had enrolled to train as a social worker.

The case of *Venables and Thompson v News Group Newspapers* (2001) showed what was possible when a judge felt impelled to act against media intrusion. The case concerned the killers of Jamie Bulger, imprisoned since they were children and about to be released into what might have been a media feeding frenzy and could have culminated in a lynching. The President of the Family Division granted an indefinite injunction against publication of details of their whereabouts. Here not only privacy rights but the right to life itself were at issue. Nonetheless the decision provided some encouragement for advocates of greater judicial boldness in the privacy area.

Wainwright v Home Office (2003) represented a high level setback for the advocates of a privacy right in English law. Lord Hoffmann asserted firmly that there was no tort of invasion of privacy as such. The creation of a high-level principle of privacy would require legislation rather than broad brush common law principles. The Human Rights Act was an argument against rather than an argument for a comprehensive privacy right at common law, since it provided a statutory remedy for breaches by a public authority.

Another unsuccessful attempt to mobilise a privacy right occurred in *A v B and C* (2002), where the Court of Appeal considered a football player's appeal against the rejection of his claim for an injunction to stop publication of a kiss and tell account of his adultery. The court set out detailed guidelines but warned judges against trying to ferret out a new cause of action in privacy, stating that in the great majority of actions breach of confidence would supply adequate protection. The "vexed question" of the existence of a separate privacy tort need not be tackled.

The latest high-profile case was *Campbell v MGN* (2004), in which the House of Lords, by a three-two majority, upheld the privacy right of a fashion model with a drug problem. Naomi Campbell had falsely claimed not to take illegal drugs. The newspaper published a photograph of her leaving a Narcotics Anonymous session alongside an article revealing that she was indeed a drug addict. There was no breach of her right to privacy in the revelation that she took drugs, but the majority of the

Lords held that publication of the photographs was an unwarranted breach of her privacy. It might interfere with her treatment, and went beyond the margin of appreciation allowed to the newspaper. Even here there was powerful dissent, particularly by Lord Hoffmann who pointed out the dangers of judges acting as newspaper editors.

While English law has kept privacy rights on a short rein, the Strasbourg court has taken a much stronger line. This is evident particularly from *Peck v UK* (2003). The claimant's suicide attempt while depressed was caught on a council closed-circuit video. After the incident had been dealt with police, the council released the video for use in publicity for the effectiveness of closed circuit television. Peck unsuccessfully sought judicial review of the council's decision to release the footage, and subsequently took the case to the European Court of Human Rights, alleging *inter alia* breach of Art.8. He also claimed that Art.13 was breached by the lack of provision of an adequate remedy for the wrong that had been done to him.

The Strasbourg court held that the definition of private life was not capable of being exhaustively defined. The mere fact that the act in question occurred in public and would not have been secret to anyone in the vicinity was not a bar to protection of the right to respect for privacy. The claimant had a right to protection against wider dissemination of the footage. Disclosure of the footage was not "necessary in a democratic society" as the government had claimed. There had been no attempt to obtain his consent, nor had his identity been protected.

The government had contended that Peck had an effective remedy in the United Kingdom having regard to the regime of legal protection as a whole, rather than having regard to the absence of a general right to privacy in domestic law. An effective remedy required a competent national authority to deal with the substance of a complaint, and to grant appropriate relief. Confidence did not come into the case, so Peck could not go bring his complaint within that framework.

In *Von Hannover v Germany* (2004) the Strasbourg Court upheld a complaint from Princess Caroline of Monaco about the German courts' failure to give her adequate protection from publication of paparazzo photographs of her going about her daily life. The court held that although freedom of expression also extended to the publication of photographs, this was an area in which the protection of the rights and reputation of others took on particular importance, as it did not concern the dissemination of "ideas", but of images containing very personal or even intimate "information" about an individual.

The decisive factor in balancing protection of private life against freedom of expression lay in the contribution that the published photographs and articles made to a debate of general interest. In Caroline's photographs she was engaged in activities of a purely private nature. The general public had no legitimate interest in knowing Caroline's whereabouts or how she behaved generally in her private life.

Finally, in *Craxi v Italy* (2003) the court again showed its concern that the state should keep confidential records confidential. It held that the Italian state had failed to fulfil its positive obligations under Art.8. Its actions had led to unauthorised access to confidential files which contained recordings of intercepted phone calls. These had been published in the press. English and Havers see this as a particularly important case since, as they write, "the court not only found that it was incumbent on the state to prevent access to this information but went on to find that where unauthorised disclosure has taken place, the positive obligation inherent in the effective respect for private life implies an obligation to carry out effective inquiries into such interference with private life in order, so far as was possible, to rectify the position." English and Havers conclude that the case "seems to us to be a profoundly important step for the court to have taken in developing the scope of privacy protection under the Convention. It has given Article 8 the adjectival duty to carry out effective investigation similar to the adjectival duty which arose under Article 2."

What is clear from the cases and the different stances taken in Strasbourg and London is that privacy rights are a continuing battleground whose shape is still not fully determined. It is equally clear that in the absence of parliamentary legislation progress will be incremental, piecemeal and slow.

QUESTION 3

Harry is suing his ex-employer, a local authority, for negligence. He claims he is unable to walk properly since he injured his back in an accident at work. His employer has arranged for a surveillance agent to follow him secretly and see if he is exaggerating his injuries. Secret video film is taken of Harry jogging with his children in his garden and in the park. Does Harry have any

rights under the Human Rights Act with regard to his surveillance? Would it make any difference to your answer if Harry's
employer was a private company?

Answer

The relevant Article here is Art.8 which guarantees rights to
privacy and family life to which the English common law gave
little protection. The Strasbourg court has acknowledged that
interference by surveillance must be "in accordance with the
law". Thus in *Halford v UK* (1997), there was a violation of Art.8
when the police intercepted telephone conversations of a woman
assistant chief constable without legal authority. The purpose of
Art.8 is to protect people against invasions of privacy. Like other
Articles of the Convention the extent of the protection afforded to
individuals has developed over time. There are four protected
interests, namely private life, home and family life and correspondence.

There is no right to be simply left alone. Thus in *Niemitz v
Germany* (1993), the court commented:

> " . . . it would be too restrictive to limit the notion [of private life]
> to an inner circle in which the individual may live his own personal
> life as he chooses and to exclude therefrom entirely the outside
> world not encompassed within that circle".

However, investigations into private lives must be justified. In
Smith and Grady v UK (2000), the Strasbourg court found that
investigations conducted by the Ministry of Defence into the
sexual orientation of members of the armed services and the
dismissal of some members constituted "especially grave" interference with their private lives. Clearly here Harry has not yet
suffered a detriment such as loss of post as a result of the
surveillance, but it may be open to him to argue that by filming
him in his house the local authority was invading both his
privacy and his family life.

There is no clear definition of "family life". In *K v UK* (1986),
the Commission interpreted the meaning of family life when it
stated, "the question of the existence or non-existence of 'family
life' is essentially a question of fact depending upon the real
existence in practice of close personal ties". It is open to Harry to
argue that his ties with his children are intruded upon and thus
his family life was violated.

Similarly, Harry's home may include his garden, which will thus engage Art.8. Harry may be able to claim that intrusive videoing in his garden can possibly fall within the definition of intrusion into his private space. He is on less sure ground in relation to the videoing in the park. It would be unlikely that the definition of private space would be stretched to apply to public land. People have been routinely photographed in public and closed circuit television cameras are widespread in countries in Europe where the Convention has long been part of national law. However, there is no clear authority on this. Harry cannot claim any common law property in his image but he might be able to argue that if the surveillance amounts to blatant harassment then there should be a prosecution under the Harassment Act 1997. The application of this statute would have "as far as possible" to be carried out in the light of the Convention.

It is possible therefore that there is a breach of para.1 of Art.8. Does the breach fall within the necessary qualifications? It is arguably in accordance with law if the filming is actually carried out in a public place, *i.e.* the film maker is in the street and gets film of the garden at long distance. If however the local authority has tricked its way into Harry's house then arguably it has committed trespass and is not authorised to film.

Is the filming "necessary in a democratic society"? Here the issue of proportionality is raised and in particular if there were other less intrusive ways of finding out about Harry's condition, for example by giving him a medical examination. In general, secret filming is considered objectionable since it is not open to those who were the subject of the filming to take any action to prevent it. This was the position even before the operation of the Human Rights Act. For example, in *R. v Broadcasting Standards Commission, Ex p. British Broadcasting Corporation* (2000), the Court of Appeal found that secret filming by the BBC in a store to which the public had access was an infringement of a company's privacy. Lord Woolf considered that the relevant statute, the Broadcasting Act 1996, provided greater protection than Art.8 since it extended to companies.

More serious for Harry is the possibility under Art.8 that the filming is in the interests of "the economic well-being of the country". In *MS v Sweden* (1998), the Social Insurance office had gained access to the medical records of an applicant for compensation for a work-related injury. She was not awarded the compensation because the records revealed that the claim was not work-related. MS claimed a breach of Art.8 in the handing over of the confidential medical records. The court held that there was indeed an interference with her right to privacy under Art.8. However this interference was justified since it was with the legitimate aim of the economic well being of the country. Public funds were being protected.

Overall both UK and Strasbourg jurisprudence have taken a somewhat differing stance on whether video surveillance is a breach of Art.6. In *Jones v University of Warwick* (2003) the Court of Appeal held that covert filming of a personal injury claimant by an inquiry agent did not breach privacy rights. In *JS v UK* (1993) the commission rejected a complaint that covert surveillance by an insurance company was a breach of Art.8. However, the claim was rejected not because of the nature of the alleged intrusion but because the insurance company's activities did not engage the responsibility of the state. However, *Peck v UK* (2003) is a more recent example where a breach of Art.8(1) was found to be unjustifiable, even though the objective was legitimate. The claimant had been captured on closed-circuit television attempting suicide by slashing his wrists in the high street. The images had been used in a campaign to show the benefits of closed circuit TV. This use of the pictures had been a disproportionate interference with P's private life and accordingly infringed his rights under Art.8. This judgment criticised the inaction of the English judiciary in this area and thus may enable Harry to prevent this evidence being used by the defence in his civil suit.

Given that Harry may have the basis of a violation of Art.8, does he have a cause of action? The local authority is a public body under s.6 of the Human Rights Act and it is unlawful for a public body "to act in a way which is incompatible with a Convention right". Harry is a victim and may sue in the appropriate court.

If Harry's employer were a private individual he would have more difficulty in pursuing a claim. He would only be able to argue his Art.8 rights if he had a common law or statutory cause of action or as a defence in any claim. It is difficult to see how any are appropriate here unless he appeals, through a court or tribunal, the refusal of his claim to benefit. The English courts have not drawn on Art.8 to develop a new tort of privacy.

If Harry were to be charged with a criminal offence as a result of his claims for compensation he might argue that the video films of him in the garden, which arguably are obtained unlawfully, should not be admitted in evidence. He will gain little support in this argument from the early cases applying the Human Rights Act.

In *R. v Loveridge and Others* (2001), the Court of Appeal held that secret filming by the police of defendants in the cell area of a magistrate's court was unlawful and a breach of their right to privacy, which since it was not in accordance with the law could not be justified. However, a judge had been entitled to admit the film in evidence at the defendants' trial as it had not interfered with the fairness of the trial. In that case there had been a clear illegality in the filming, in particular a breach of s.41 of the Criminal Justice Act 1925. This is not the case in this instance, so Harry is unlikely to have such evidence excluded by operation of s.78 of the Police and Criminal Evidence Act 1984. Although their Lordships in *Loveridge* had given full weight to the breach of the Convention they were satisfied that the contravention of Art.8 did not interfere with the fairness of the hearing. This illustrates that in general the requirements of fairness under s.78 and Art.6 will be the same.

However, Harry may draw more comfort from the Strasbourg Court decision in *Perry v UK* (2003). There the applicant's Art.8 rights were infringed when police covertly took video pictures of him in the police station and subsequently used them in an identification procedure. The procedure adopted by the police did not comply with the Codes of Practice under the Police and Criminal Evidence Act 1984, s.66. In general however the Strasbourg Court holds that the operation of the rules of evidence is a matter for the national courts and even where breaches of Art.8 are found this does not necessarily mean that the evidence should not be admitted (see *Khan v UK* (2000)).

QUESTION 4

The government is considering bringing in a measure which would require 16–18 year olds to work for a charity organisation for one week without payment, in their summer holidays. If they refuse some family social security benefit will be denied to the family. Advise whether such legislation will be potentially in breach of the European Convention on Human Rights.

Answer

The Key Articles here are Art.4 and to a lesser extent Art.8. Article 4 is one of just a handful of rights in the Convention which are absolute or unqualified (the others being 2, 3, 4, 7, 12 and 14). Such rights are accorded high status. Thus, for example in *Chahal v UK* (1997), the Strasbourg court held that it was a violation of Art.3 to refuse asylum to a man who risked ill-treatment if he was deported to India. The court so held that, although the man was a potential danger in the UK because of his terrorist activities. Critics of this decision argued that it involved giving a higher value to the interests of the terrorist than to those of vulnerable nationals. The case thus illustrates that applications under these Articles which give absolute rights are treated with full seriousness. In the light of this it is difficult on the facts given in the question to see how Art.4 could be applicable.

Article 4 guarantees freedom from slavery, servitude or forced or compulsory labour. Only a very few cases have been brought under this Article and only one breach has been found. This however was mainly on the grounds of sex-discrimination in a case where the government required only men, not women, to serve in the fire brigade or make a payment instead (see *Karlheinz Schmidt v Germany* (1994)). Cases which have been dismissed as manifestly ill founded include *Harper v UK* (1986), concerning the compulsory retirement age, and *X v UK* (1969), concerning compulsory labour in prison.

The Article bans slavery, servitude or compulsory labour. Slavery and servitude clearly do not apply here. Does forced or compulsory labour? The court applies the definition provided by the Conventions of the International Labour Office, in particular Art.2 of ILO Convention No 29. This defines "compulsory labour" as "all work or service which is exacted from any person under the menace of any penalty and for which the said person has not offered himself voluntarily". Applying this definition it did not find a violation of Art.4(2) in *Van der Mussele v Belgium* (1983). In that case the applicant, a young Belgian lawyer, claimed that the requirement to represent poor defendants for free amounted to "forced or compulsory labour". The court applied the following tests:

(a) Was the work outside the normal duties of a barrister?
(b) Did the provision of services contribute to professional development?
(c) Was the work overly burdensome?

It found no violation on these grounds. In any event it was open to the lawyer to leave the legal profession. However it was part of the reasoning of the court in this case that the requirement to offer free services on the part of young lawyers was a way of providing counsel as required under Art.6(3)(c) of the Convention. Clearly this does not apply to the problem under discussion. But the requirement that young people should do a form of community service could be said to be "a normal civic obligation" under Art.4(3)(d). The Convention is a "living instrument" and it may be that such a form of community service will be regarded as the twenty-first century equivalent of conscription or military service, which is excluded from the definition of forced labour and thus be acceptable.

On the other hand, some commentators have seen a wider application for Art.4. Thus, for example. Professor Hepple has suggested that Art.4(2) may be applicable in relation to welfare benefits. He cites the hypothetical case where, for example, a job-seekers' allowance is not payable where a claimant has without good cause refused or failed to carry out a job-seekers' direction which was reasonable having regard to the claimant's circumstances. Hepple writes: "An obligation to work as a condition of receiving welfare benefits may leave the able-bodied objector with only the freedom to starve". It does not appear here that the family would have no income but it might be arguable that undue compulsion is put on the 16–18 year olds.

However, one problem in applying Art.4 in this instance is that the English courts are not enthusiastic about applying absolute rights. For example, in *North-West Lancashire Health Authority v A, D and G* (2000), the Court of Appeal dismissed an application to apply Art.3, which protects against cruel and unusual treatment in a situation where transsexuals had been refused a sex change operation. Buxton L.J. said:

> "Article 3 of the European Convention on Human Rights addresses positive conduct by public officials of a high degree of seriousness and opprobrium. It has never been applied to merely policy decisions on the allocation of resources".

And he added:

> " . . . to attempt to bring the present case under Article 3 not only strains language and commonsense, but also and even more seriously trivialises that Article in relation to the very important values that it in truth protects".

Again, in *R. v Daniels* (2000), the Court of Appeal stated that it was essential that counsel, those who instructed counsel as to when it was right to raise arguments based on the Human Rights Act 1978 and judges should be robust in resisting inappropriate attempts to introduce such arguments.

It does not appear that Art.4 itself has been raised in any cases under the Human Rights Act however the likely approach of the courts may perhaps be judges from the restrictive approach to Arts 2 and 3. For example, in *R. (Q and Others) v Secretary of State for the Home Department* (2003) the Court of Appeal held that there would be a violation of Art.3 if there was a real risk that injury to health would arise. However, Art.3 and Art.8 were not breached in this case. It may be worth considering whether there is a potential breach of Art.8 in this legislation. The courts have recently been more robust in identifying Art.8 breaches as for example in the House of Lords decision in *R. (Razgar) v Secretary of State for the Home Department* (2003).

In conclusion therefore it is likely that this statutory provision does not violate Art.4 and the Minister is likely to come to the conclusion that she may make a statement of compatibility.

QUESTION 5

a) Section 61 of the Criminal Justice and Public Order Act 1994 creates an offence of trespass and in s.61(6) specifies that:

> " . . . in proceedings from an offence under this section it is a defence for the accused to show (a) that he was not trespassing on the land, or (b) that he had a reasonable excuse for failing to leave the land as soon as reasonably practicable or, as the case may be, for again entering the land".

Jerry is charged with an offence under this section. He fails to give an explanation as to why he was on the land. Advise him as to whether he will gain assistance in his defence from Art.6 of the European Convention on Human Rights.

Answer

Article 6(2) reads: "Everyone charged with a criminal offence shall be presumed innocent until proved guilty according to law". This reflects the English common law position contained in *Woolmington v DPP* (1935), where Lord Sankey in the House of Lords said:

> "No matter what the charge or where the trial, the principle that the prosecution must prove the guilt of the prisoner is part of the

common law of England and no attempt to whittle it down can be entertained".

However, Woolmington also recognised exceptions to this "golden thread", including express statutory exceptions. In other words, Parliament could expressly reverse the burden of proof. This situation, however, must now be looked at in the light of s.3 of the Human Rights Act, which requires that "so far as it is possible to do so, primary legislation must be read and given effect in a way which is compatible with Convention rights".

However, Jerry should be advised that the Strasbourg court has not recognised the placing of the burden of proof on the prosecution as being an absolute rule. Thus, for example, in *Salabiaku v France* (1988), the applicant had been convicted of smuggling prohibited goods under Art.392(1) of the French Customs Code. Under this code, if the prosecution proved that the defendant was in possession of the goods at issue then the defendant was liable. The court did not regard this imposition of strict liability as a violation of Art.6, but it also stated:

> "Article 6(2) does not therefore regard presumptions of fact or of law provided for in the criminal law with indifference. It requires states to confine them within reasonable limits which take into account the importance of what is at stake and maintain the rights of the defence".

It was significant that in this specific case the defendant did have some means of defence. Under French law there was a certain amount of discretion in assessing the evidence and so it was at least in principle possible to find for a defendant and not impose strict liability.

The approach of the English courts was shown in *R. v DPP, Ex p. Kebilene* (1999), where the House of Lords considered a section of the Prevention of Terrorism (Temporary Provisions) Act 1989 which shifted the burden of proof. The Divisional Court had considered that this section was incompatible with Art.6(2). The House of Lords did not see the need to make a ruling on that issue but did consider it. Lord Hope of Craighead stated that the statute should be analysed to see whether it shifted the legal burden, that is the burden of convicting the trier of fact at the end of the trial or simply the lesser evidential burden, the burden of "passing the judge" or getting the matter discussed at trial.

Even if the provision imposes a legal burden then a pragmatic approach should be adopted to see if the section is compatible with the Convention. This included asking how heavy the burden was, what was the mischief the provision was designed to address and was the burden on the accused something which was likely to be in his knowledge and to which he has access.

The House of Lords by a majority has now held that it may not be justifiable to use s.28 of the Misuse of Drugs Act 1971 so as to transfer the legal burden to the accused. It was possible to construe s.28 as imposing an evidential rather a legal burden and such a requirement was not a violation of the Convention. Lord Steyn argued for outlawing reverse burdens where the defence bears directly on the moral blameworthiness of the defendant. An important factor was the seriousness of the offence charged. The decision does not mean that parliament can never put a burden of proof on a defendant. For example, in *L v DPP* (2002) the Divisional Court held that s.139(4) of the Criminal Justice Act 1988 placed a legal burden on the defendant "to prove that he had good reason or lawful authority for having (an offensive weapon) with him in a public place." The issue for Jerry therefore is how the courts will interpret s.61(6). Guidance is given by the House of Lords case in *R. v Johnstone* (2003) and by the Court of Appeal in *Attorney-General's reference* (No.1 of 2004). It was held in both cases that both the common law and Art.6(2) permitted reverse burdens in appropriate circumstances so long as they were confined within reasonable limits and took account of the importance of what was at stake and maintained the rights of the defence. Reverse legal burdens, the standard of proof being the civil standard, were probably justified if the overall burden remained on the prosecution but parliament had for significant resons concluded that it was fair and reasonable to make an exception in respect of a particular aspect of the offence.

In this instance it might be argued that the reverse burdens placed on the defendant in order to establish a defence fall within the "reasonable limits" set out in *Salabiaku*. Jerry is best placed to know if he had a legitimate reason for being on the land, that does not seem a heavy burden to discharge and the Criminal Justice and Public Order Act was designed, *inter alia*, to deal with the social problem of mass trespass by New Age Travellers, hunt saboteurs, etc. (see *R. (Fuller) v Chief Constable Dorset* (2001)).

b) Contraltos Ltd, a waste-management operation, are unlawfully dumping poisonous waste on land owned by Wessex County Council. The council had received a report from the local University Environmental Science Department indicating that fumes from this waste matter may cause skin damage in children.

Children have been playing on the nearby wasteland and several of them have developed unpleasant skin problems. Advise whether the children have any rights under the Human Rights Act additional to their common law or statutory rights under English law.

Answer

The situation may involve infringements of the right to respect for private and family life (Art.8). Environmental pollution can be a violation of Art.8. In *Baggs, Powell and Raynor v UK* (1990), noise from Heathrow created a nuisance. The Commission noted:

> " . . . Considerable noise nuisance can undoubtedly affect the physical well-being of a person and thus interfere with his private life. It may also deprive a person of the possibility of enjoying the amenities of his home".

However, the interference in this instance was not disproportionate to the legitimate aim of running the airport.

More recently the Strasbourg Court had taken a more restrictive view of environmental rights under Art.8. Thus the Grand Chamber of the Strasbourg Court decided in *Hatton v UK* (2003) that there was no infringement of Art.8. The case arose from the implementation of a new night flight scheme at Heathrow. The applicants claimed this had led to an increase in night-time aircraft noise. The court held that environmental protection had no special status under the Convention and that this was a case where the state's margin of appreciation in the light of policy decisions should be given special weight. The approach of the English courts to environmental issues has been similarly narrow. In *Marcic v Thames Water Utilities* (2003) the House of Lords emphasised the importance of public policy over the interests of individuals in environmental issues. In the Court of Appeal Marcic had succeeded under the common law on the basis that sewage coming onto his land was an actionable nuisance. The Court of Appeal approved of the trial judge's references to Protocol 1, Art.1 of the ECHR. The House of Lords disagreed with this approach and held it was for parliament and administrators to determine such issues. These decisions indicate that the children or their representatives cannot rely on environmental rights being given a particular status under the Human Rights Act.

Here, if we assume that the pollution is sufficiently serious to affect the physical well being of local children, it cannot be said to have arisen in pursuit of a legitimate aim, since, as we are told, it has been generated unlawfully, but Contraltos Ltd is not a public authority and it is doubtful whether the Human Rights Act gives victims of the pollution it has generated any cause of action against it beyond those such as nuisance and breach of statutory duty available prior to the passage of the Human Rights Act.

A relevant public authority is Wessex County Council whose land is being used for unlawful dumping. It is not clear whether there is any relationship between Contraltos and the Council. If, for example, the waste-management company were carrying out public waste-disposal functions on the authority's behalf, the authority might be susceptible to legal action for having delegated its functions to a company which was carrying them out improperly, and in the process infringing the Convention rights of local families.

It is not clear from the question whether the children, their parents or guardians have seen the report indicating that fumes may harm children's skin. If the council is withholding the details of the risk to health it risks action under Article 8. The key case here is *Guerra v Italy* (1998). In that case pollution from a chemical factory a mile from the applicant's home provided grounds for a violation of Art.8, since the authorities had not provided relevant information about the risks to their health. There was a positive obligation to inform local people about health matters in "circumstances which foreseeably and on substantial grounds present a real risk of danger to heath and physical integrity".

It is important to note that the "circumstances" do not have to have been the result of government or public authority action. The issue is whether they had the power to stop the situation and did not do so (see *L.C.B. v UK* (1998)). Another case on information about health risks is *McGinley and Egan v UK* (1998). The applicants in that case had served at Christmas Island during the nuclear tests. Article 8 applied because:

> " . . . given the fact that exposure to high levels of radiation is known to have hidden but serious and long-lasting effects on health, it is not unnatural that the applicants' uncertainty as to whether or not they had been put at risk in this way caused them substantial anxiety and distress . . . since the [radiation level records] contained information which might have assisted the applicants in assessing radiation levels in the areas in which they

were stationed during the tests, they had an interest under Article 8 in obtaining access to them".

There was a positive obligation under Art.8:

"Where a government engages in hazardous activities, such as those in issue in the present case, which might have hidden adverse consequences on the health of those involved in such activities, respect for private and family life under Article 8 requires that an effective and accessible procedure be established which enables persons to seek all relevant and appropriate information".

It may be arguable that Art.2 is also engaged, although the Strasbourg case law has limited the scope of this article to the right to have a physical life rather than a right to enjoy life free from the effects of pollution. In some other jurisdictions, notably that of India, the right to life has included the right of enjoyment of pollution-free water and air. Notably, although this view did not form part of the majority decision in *Guerra*, one judge thought that the facts of the case raised the issue of Art.2 also, in that there was a real risk of danger to health and physical integrity. However, the council might well argue that the case law suggests that Art.2 claims are to be treated cautiously. For example, in *Osman v UK* (1998), the court referred to the need to avoid imposing "an impossible or disproportionate burden on the authorities" and that "not every claimed risk to life can entail for the authorities a convention requirement to take operational measures to prevent that risk from materialising". Nonetheless, it is not difficult to accept that the council should have acted with more vigour to stop the dumping and warn the children. Thus, here the children, or their next friends, may be able to argue that both Arts 8 and 2 have been violated by the council. It is possible that these arguments may also be put in an application for judicial review for an order for the dumping to be stopped by the council.

Useful websites

Council of Europe
  http://www.coe.int/DefaultEN.asp
European Court of Human Rights case-base:
  http://www.echr.coe.int/Eng/Judgments.htm
Court Service:
  http://www.courtservice.gov.uk/
Human Rights Unit, Department of Constitutional Affairs:
  http://www.humanrights.gov.uk/
Parliamentary Joint Committee on Human Rights:
  http://www.parliament.uk/parliamentary_committees/joint_committee_on_human_rights. cfm
Liberty guide to the Human Rights Act:
  http://www.yourrights.org.uk/
Home Office Study Guide to the Human Rights Act:
  http://www.dca.gov.uk/hract/study.pdf
British Council human rights material:
  http://humanrights.britishcouncil.org/
Human Rights First (formerly the Lawyers' Committee for Human Rights):
  http://www.humanrightsfirst.org/
United Nations, New York:
  http://www.un.org/rights/
United Nations High Commissioner for Human Rights, Geneva:
  http://www.ohchr.org/english/
These sites were available in July 2004, but their addresses may change in the future.

INDEX